P-51D Mustang American Aces*

Artur Juszczak

To Ewa and Krzyś.

*A **flying ace** is a military aviator credited with shooting down several enemy aircraft during aerial combat. The actual number of aerial victories required to officially qualify as an "ace" has varied, but is usually considered to be five or more.

Introduction

The P-51D Mustang, with bubble canopy, was the best-known version of the North American Aviation (NAA) Mustang. It was also the most widely used variant of the aircraft, with a total of 8102 machines of this type produced, 6502 at Inglewood and 1600 in Dallas.

The P-51B and P-51C were excellent aircraft that served until the end of the war, but B and C models suffered poor rear visibility and gun jamming during high-G manoeuvres. Also, the B/C versions only had four 0.50 in calibre Browning machine guns (two in each wing). NAA also took the opportunity to make other improvements to the new version.

The British had developed a bubble or "teardrop" canopy with 360° view and they were beginning to use them on the latest model of Spitfires and Typhoons. The U.S. Army sent Col. Mark Bradley to England in January of 1943 to learn the workings of this new canopy and then find a way to introduce them on U.S. fighters. Bradley returned and began to incorporate the new style. The first U.S. fighter so tested was a Republic P-47.

A P-51B-1 (43-12102) was selected to be modified as the test aircraft for the new bubble canopy. The new – shaped canopy gave almost completely unobstructed all-round vision with virtually no distortion from the free-blown glazing. The plexiglas of the hood was mounted on rubber in a metal frame, the sill around the bottom being very deep. The canopy was manually opened and closed by a hand crank operated by the pilot. To accommodate the new canopy, the rear fuselage of the Mustang had to be cut down, but the amount of retooling needed to accomplish this was not extensive. This modified P-51B took off on its first flight at Inglewood on 17 November 1943, with test pilot Bob Chilton at the controls.

With the success of 43-12102, NAA modified the next two P-51B-10NA serials 43-106539 and 43-106540 as NA-106 (order dated 1 May 1943) with the bubble canopy and the six 0.50 in calibre guns. These aircraft were designated P-51D-NA. These aircraft were also powered with the same engine as the P-51B/C – the Packard V-1650-7.

The gun installation was completely redesigned, to accommodate installation of three MG53-2 0.50 in calibre machine guns in each wing, all of them mounted upright and all fed by ammunition belts. The arrangement of the ammunition chutes eliminated the jamming problem of the B/C models. The inner gun carried 400 rounds and the two outer guns had 280 rounds each.

The landing gear operation was also changed and this led to an increase of the wing root chord. The aileron effectiveness and strength were both improved. A seal was added to the leading edge of the aileron which helped ease stick pressure during high speed manoeuvres. The landing light was also moved from the wing leading edge to inside the landing gear well.

The extra long-range tank behind the pilot exacerbated an existing problem with yaw stability. Also, problems had been encountered with snap-rolls causing a failure of the horizontal stabiliser on the P-51B/C and D models. As a sol most P-51D had a dorsal fin fillet added to the fuselage-vertical stabiliser join was also added to other P-51 models already in the field.

Acknowledgements

I would like to thanks for the help in making this book the following pe
Robert Pęczkowski – for the research;
Dariusz Karnas – for the excellent scale plans;
Dariusz Grzywacz – for same emblems drawings.

P-51D-5-NA Mustang, sn 44-13421, HO•P, 328th **FS (Fighter Squadron), 352**nd **FG (Fighter Group), 8**th **AF (Air Force). Bodney, UK, June 1944.**

Maj. George E. Preddy Jr., P-51 air victories – 23.83, all air victories – 26.83.

Silver/natural metal overall (See drawing 45). Mid Blue nose. D-Day stripes on wings and lower fuselage. Codes black. No dorsal fin fillet.

P-51D-25-NA Mustang, sn 44-15459, HL•B, 308th FS, 31st FG, 15th AF.
East Wretham, UK, March 1945

Capt. John J. Voll, P-51 air victories – 21, all air victories – 21.

Silver/natural metal overall. Spinner and nose red. Anti-glare panel Olive Drab.
Red stripes on tail. Yellow and red stripes on wings and horizontal stabilizer. Codes black.

P-51D-25-NA Mustang, HL•B, sn 44-15459, 308th FS, 31st FG, 15th AF.

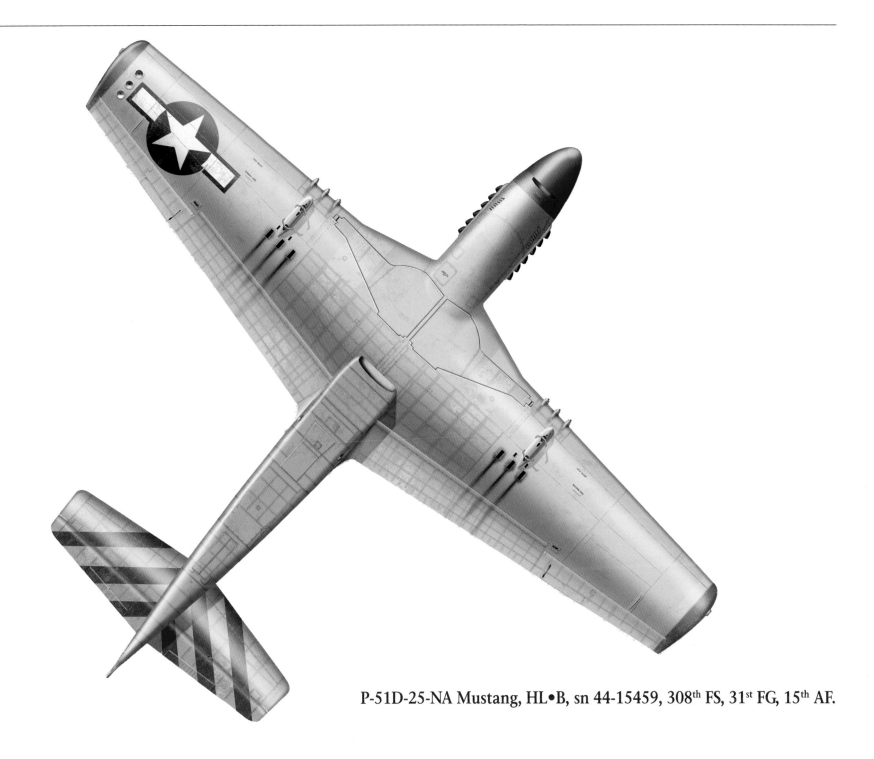

P-51D-25-NA Mustang, HL•B, sn 44-15459, 308th FS, 31st FG, 15th AF.

P-51D-25-NA Mustang, sn 44-15459, HL•B, 308th FS, 31st FG, 15th AF.

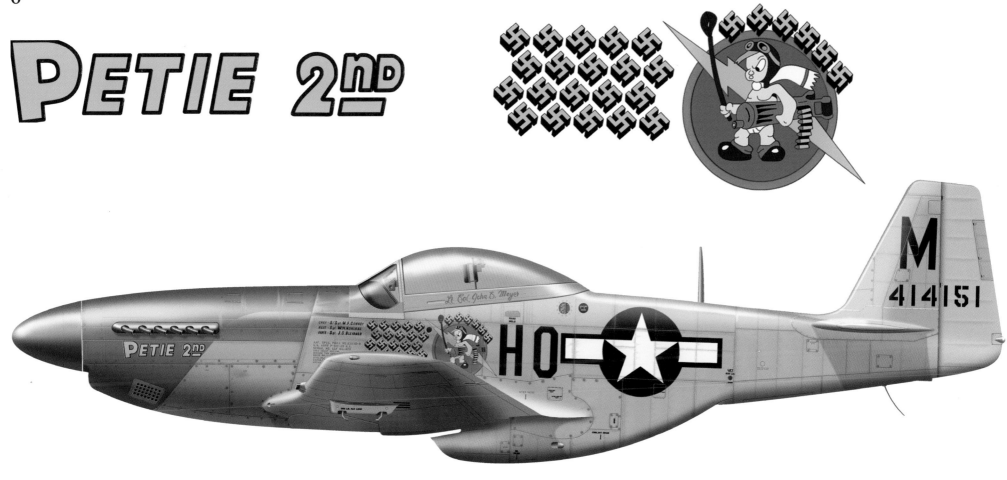

P-51D-10-NA Mustang, sn 44-14151, HO•M, 487th FS, 352nd FG, 8th AF. England, October 1944.

Lt. Col. John C. Meyer, P-51 air victories – 21, all air victories – 24.

Silver/natural metal overall. Propeller spinner and fuselage Medium Blue. Codes black. No dorsal fin fillet.

P-51D-5-NA Mustang, sn 44-13316, G4•C, 362ⁿᵈ FS, 357ᵗʰ FG, 8ᵗʰ AF. Leiston (UK), 1944.

Maj. Leonard K. Carson, P-51 air victories – 18.50, all air victories – 18.50.

Silver/natural metal overall. Upper surfaces Olive Drab. Spinner and group markings red and yellow. D-Day stripes on wings and fuselage.
White bands on horizontal stabilizer. Codes black. No dorsal fin fillet.

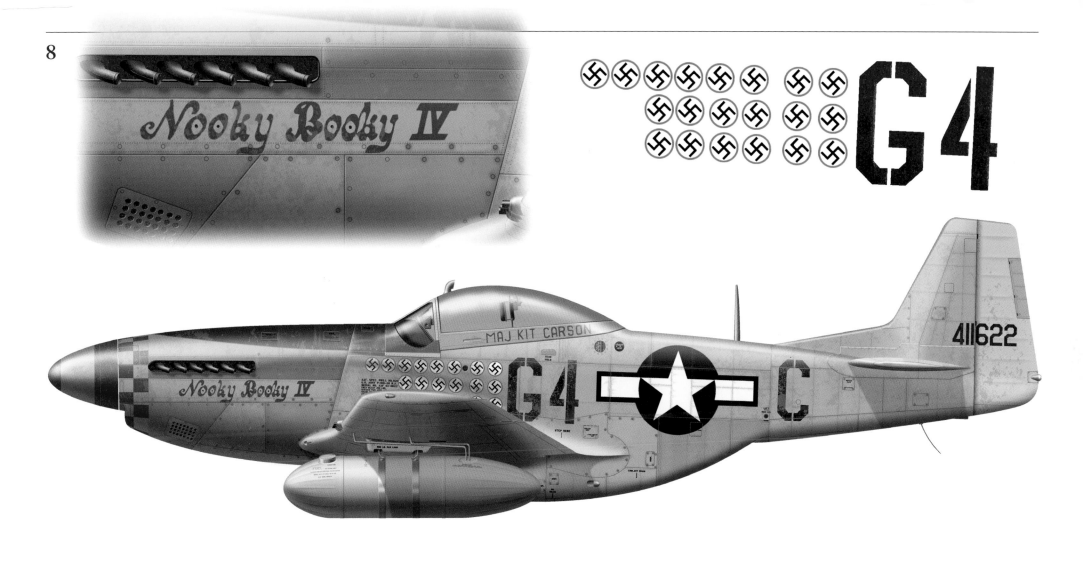

P-51K-5-NT Mustang, sn 44-11622, G4•C, 362nd FS, 357th FG, 8th AF. England, May 1945.
Maj. Leonard K. Carson, P-51 air victories – 18.50, all air victories – 18.50.
Silver/natural metal overall. Anti-glare panel Olive Drab. Spinner and group markings red and yellow. Codes black.

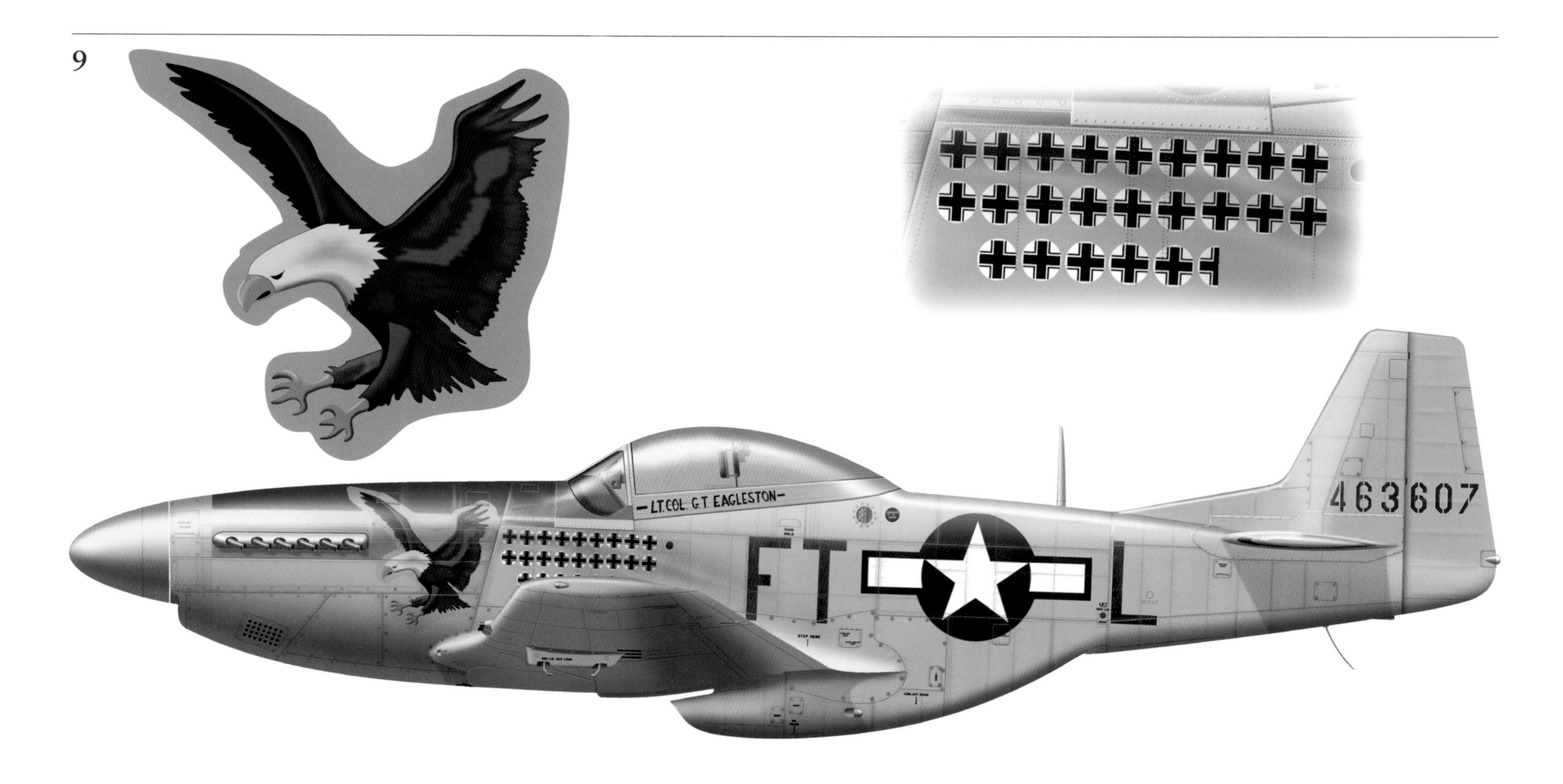

P-51D-20-NA Mustang, sn 44-63607, FT•L, 353rd FS, 354th FG, 8th AF.
Ober Olm, Germany, April 1945.
Maj. Glenn T. Eagleston, P-51 air victories – 18.50, all air victories – 18.50.
Silver/natural metal overall. Anti-glare panel Olive Drab. Spinner and group markings yellow. Black bands on horizontal stabilizer. Codes black.

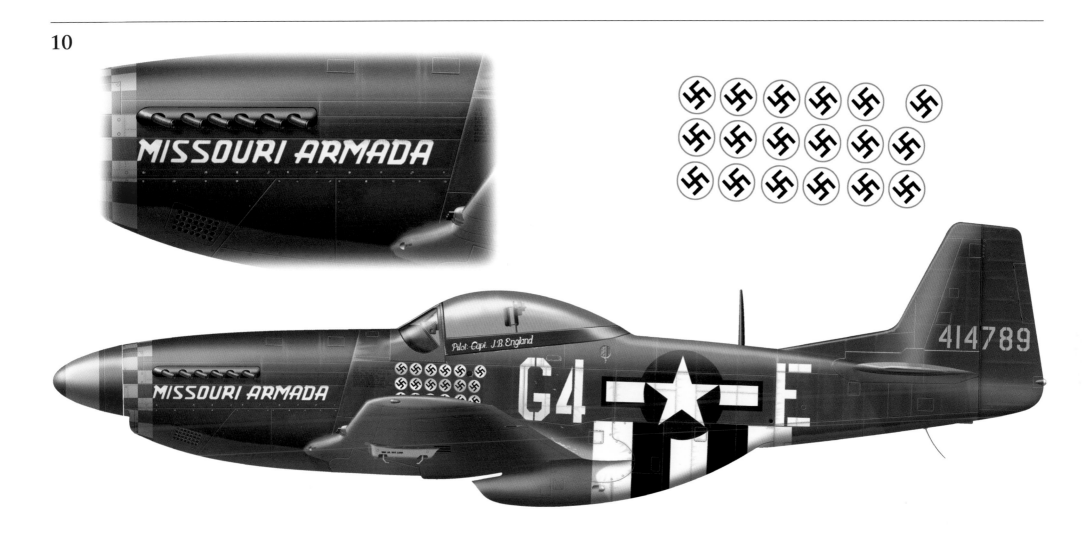

P-51D-10-NA Mustang, sn 44-14789, G4•E, 362nd FS, 357th FG, 8th AF. England, December 1944.

Maj. John B. England, P-51 air victories – 17.50, all air victories – 17.50.

Upper surfaces Olive Drab, under surfaces Natural Grey. Spinner and group markings red and yellow. D-Day stripes on lower fuselage only. Codes white. Serial Yellow.

Capt. Sully Varnell

DALEBROUX   JONES   FLEMING

AAF. SPEC. PROJ. NO.9254-R
U.S. ARMY P-51D-5 N.A.
SERIAL NO. AAF 44-13431
CREW WEIGHT 200 LBS
SERVICE THIS AND
GRADE 100/
AVAILABLE
CONSULTE
SUITABL

LITTLE EVA III

413431

P-51D-5-NA Mustang, sn 44-13431, QP•E, 2nd FS, 52nd FG, 15th AF. Italy, 1944.

Capt. James S. Varnell Jr., P-51 air victories – 17, all air victories – 17.

Silver/natural metal overall. Anti-glare panel Olive Drab. Spinner and nose red. Yellow stripes with black outline on wings and fuselage. Codes red. Serial black.
No dorsal fin fillet.

P-51D-25-NA Mustang, sn 44-72934, VF•T, 4ᵗʰ FG, 8ᵗʰ AF. War Bond Tour in US, 1944.

Capt. Don S. Gentile, P-51 air victories – 16.50, all air victories – 21.83.

Silver/natural metal overall. Anti-glare panel Olive Drab. Spinner and nose red. White and red checker. Rudder red. Codes black.

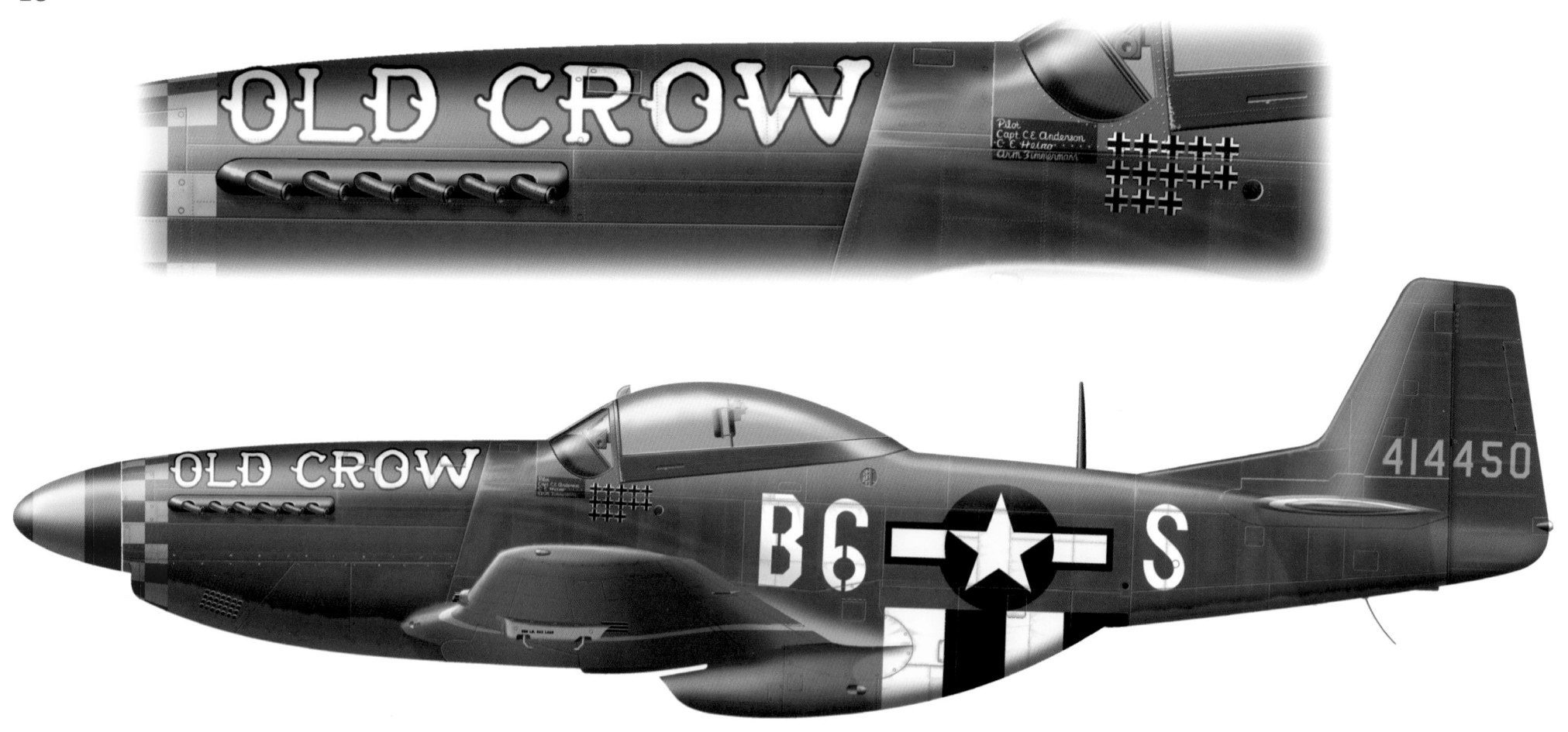

P-51D-10-NA Mustang, sn 44-14450, B6•S, 363rd FS, 357th FG, 8th AF. Leiston, UK, 1944.

Capt. Clarence E. Anderson Jr., P-51 air victories – 16.25, all air victories – 21.25.

Upper surfaces Olive Drab, under surfaces Natural Grey. Spinner and group markings red and yellow. D-Day stripes on lower fuselage only.
White bands on wings and horizontal stabilizer. Codes white. Serial yellow.

P-51D-10-NA Mustang, sn 44-14450, B6•S, 363rd FS, 357th FG, 8th AF. Leiston, UK, Winter 1944.

Capt. Clarence E. Anderson Jr., P-51 air victories – 16.25, all air victories – 21.25.

Silver/natural metal overall. Anti-glare panel Olive Drab. Spinner and group markigs red and yellow. D-Day stripes on lower fuselage only. Rudder red. Black bands on wings and horizontal stabilizer. Codes black. Serial black and yellow.

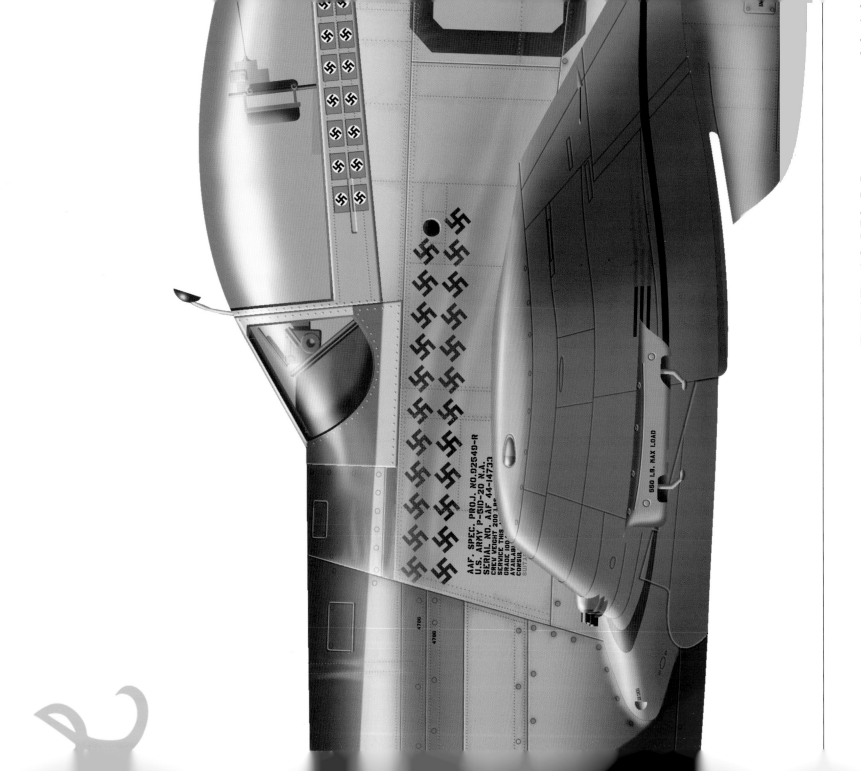

P-51D-10-NA Mustang, sn 44-14

Capt. Ray S. Wetmore, P-51 Air Vic

Silver/natural metal overall. Anti-glare panel Olive Drab. Spinner and nose green. Rud

AAF. SPEC. PROJ. NO.92549-R
U.S. ARMY P-51D-20 N.A.
SERIAL NO. AAF 44-14733
CREW WEIGHT 200 LB.
SERVICE THIS
GRADE 100
AVAILABL
CONSUL
SUITA

550 LB. MAX LOAD

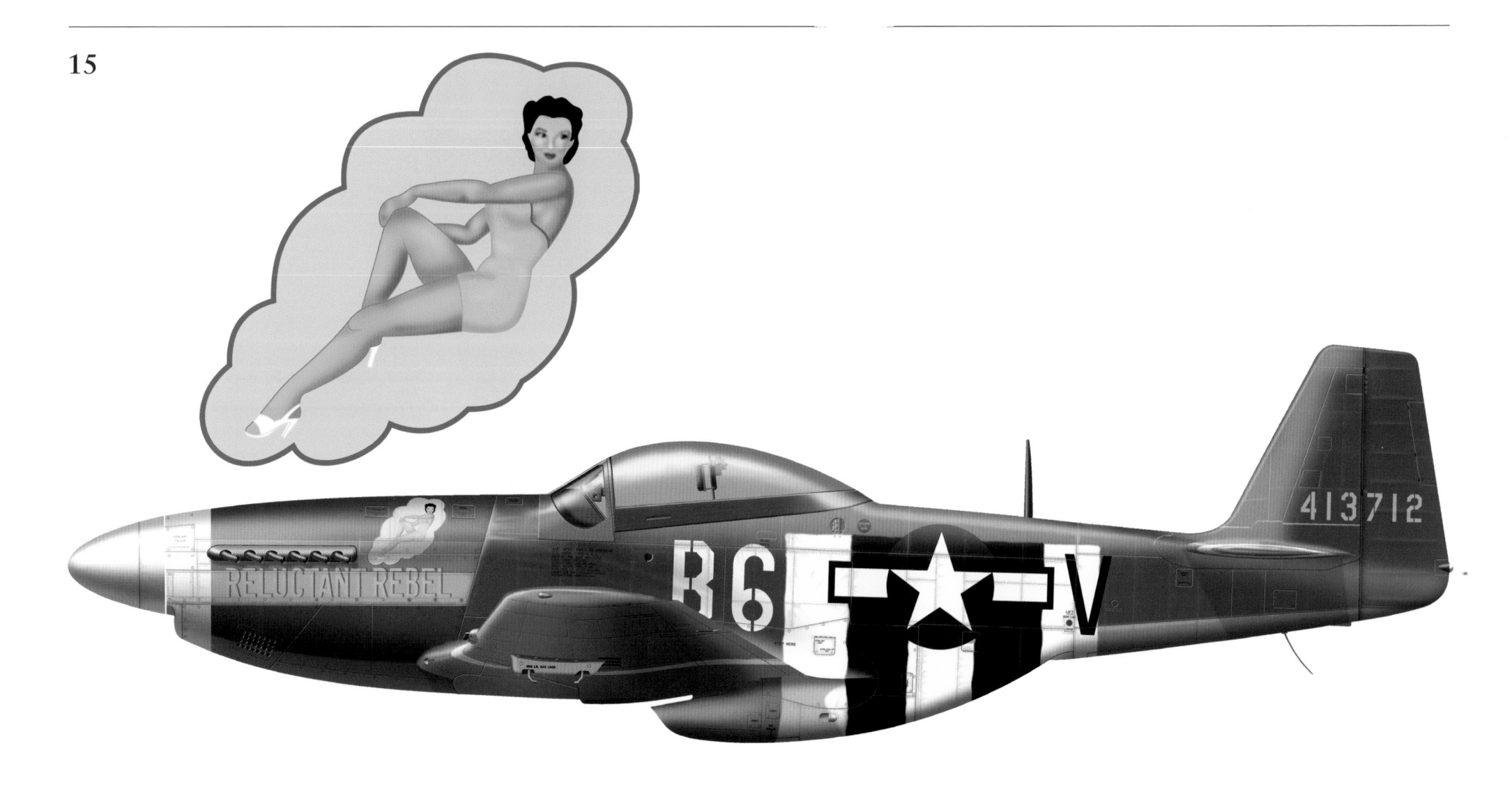

P-51D-5-NA Mustang, sn 44-13712, B6•V, 363rd FS, 357th FG, 8th AF. England, July 1944.

Maj. Robert W. Foy, P-51 air victories – 15, all air victories – 15.

Upper surfaces Dark Green, under surfaces Medium Sea Grey. Spinner and nose white. D-Day stripes on fuselage. White bands on wings and horizontal stabilizer.
Codes white and black. Serial Yellow. No dorsal fin fillet.

P-51D-5-NA Mustang, sn 44-13712, B6•V, 363rd FS, 357th FG, 8th AF

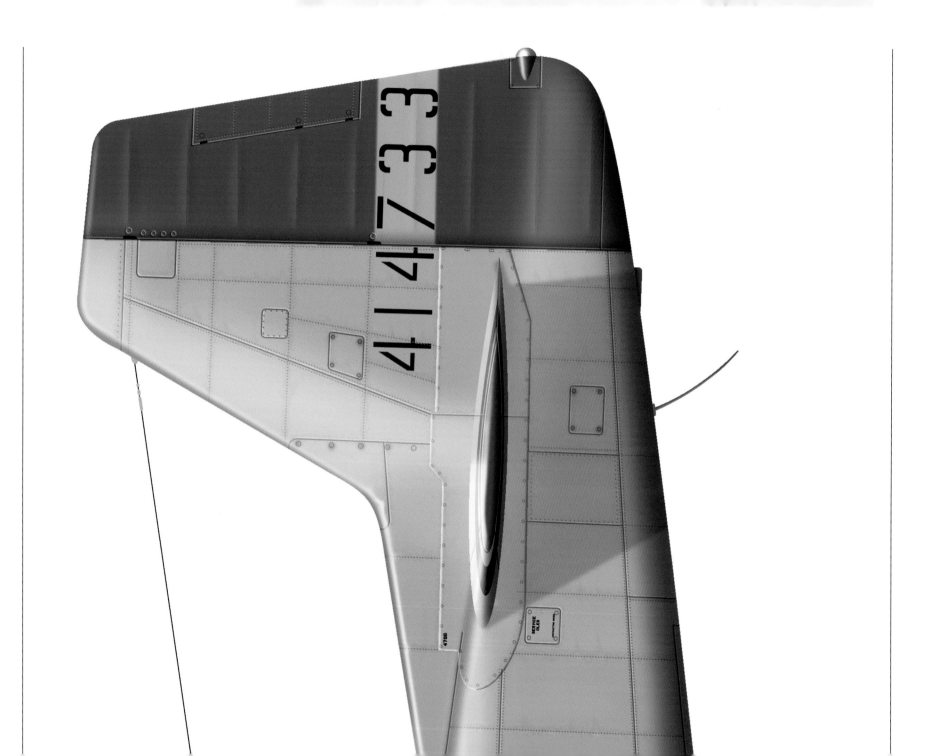

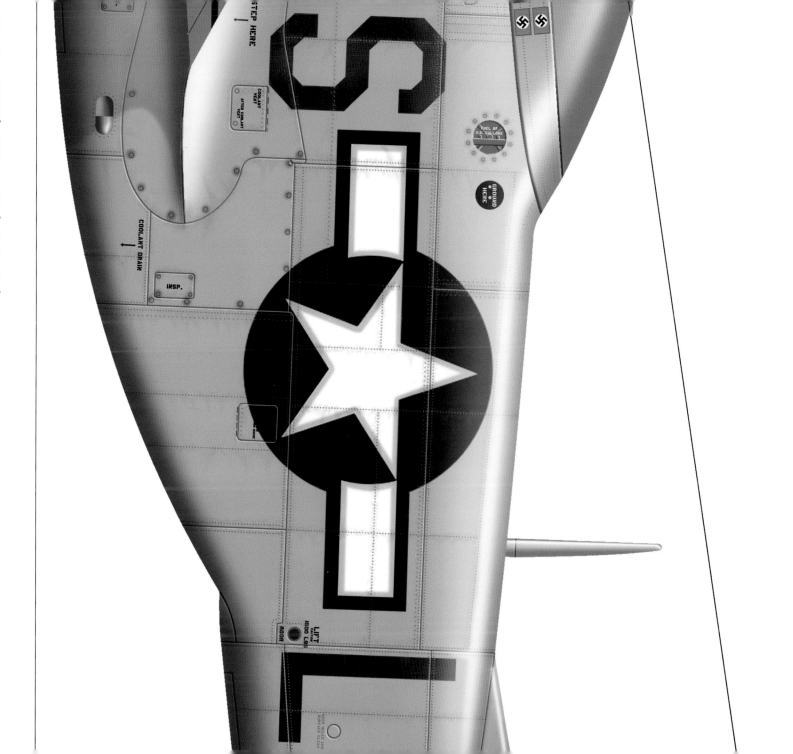

CS•L, 370th FS, 357th FG, 8th AF
– 17.00, All Air Victories – 21.25.
Black bands on wings. Black and blue bands on horizontal stabilizer. Codes black.

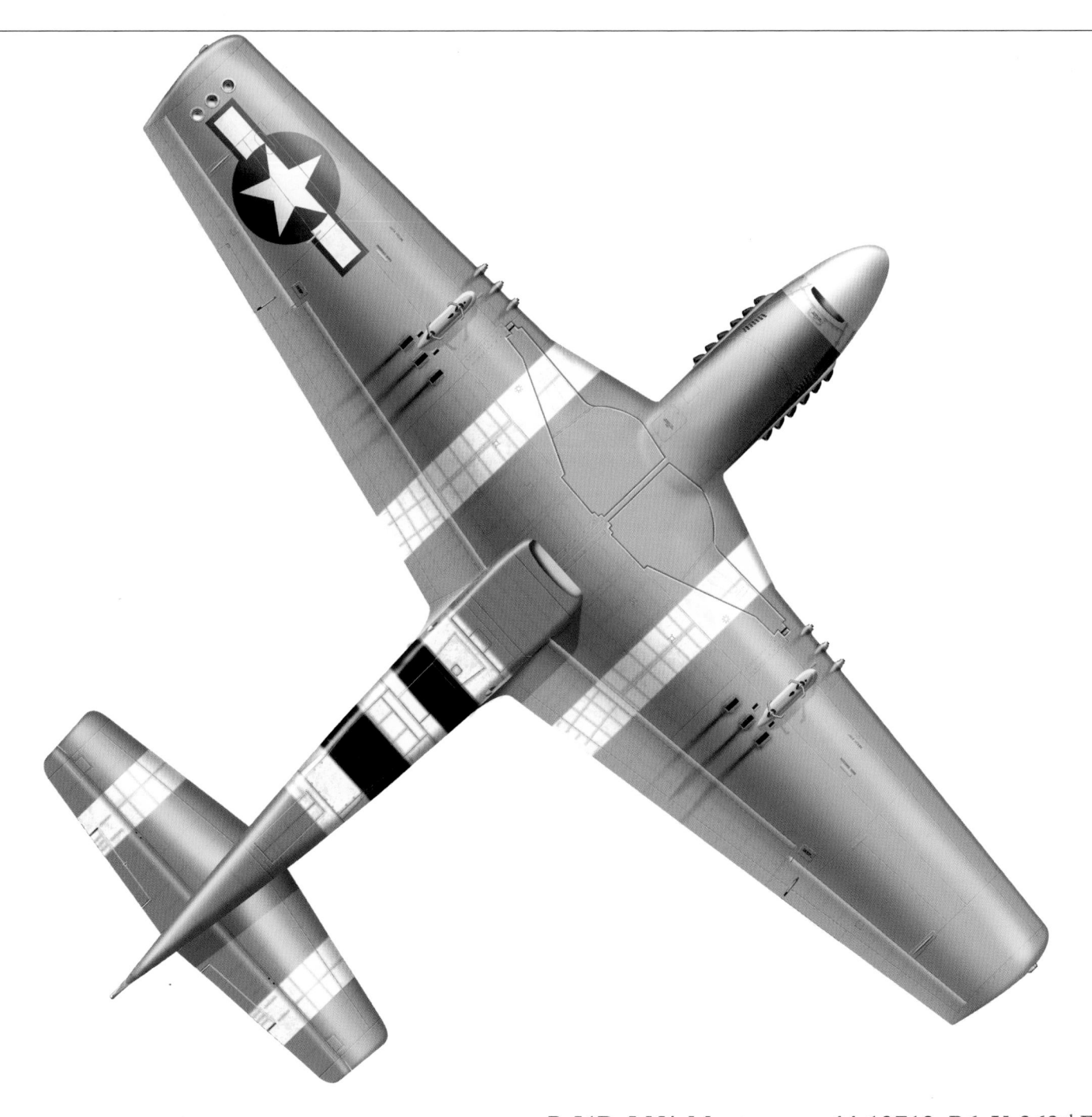

P-51D-5-NA Mustang, sn 44-13712, B6•V, 363rd FS, 357th FG, 8th AF

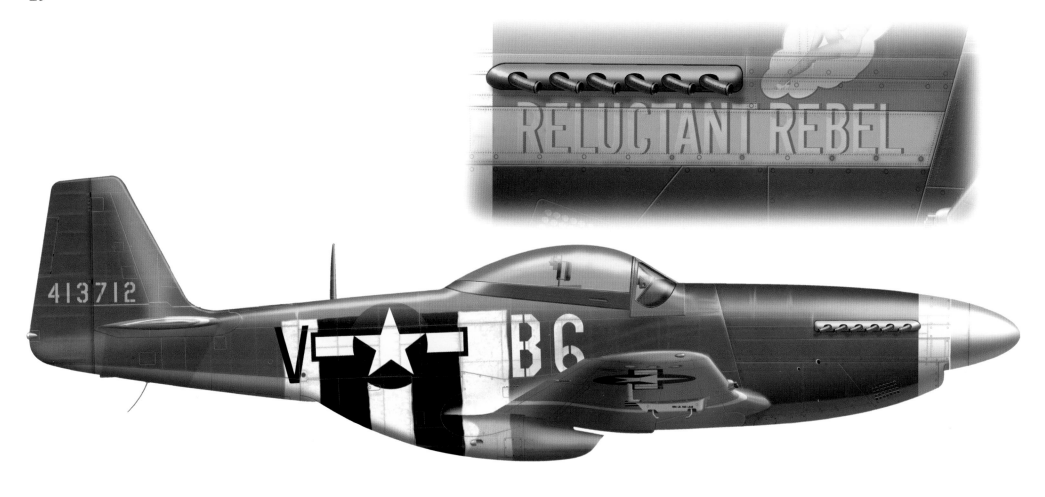

P-51D-5-NA Mustang, sn 44-13712, B6•V, 363rd FS, 357th FG, 8th AF. England, July 1944.

Maj. Robert W. Foy, P-51 air victories – 15, all air victories – 15.

Upper surfaces Dark Green, under surfaces Medium Sea Grey. Spinner and nose white. D-Day stripes on fuselage. White bands on wings and horizontal stabilizer. Codes white and black. Serial Yellow. No dorsal fin fillet.

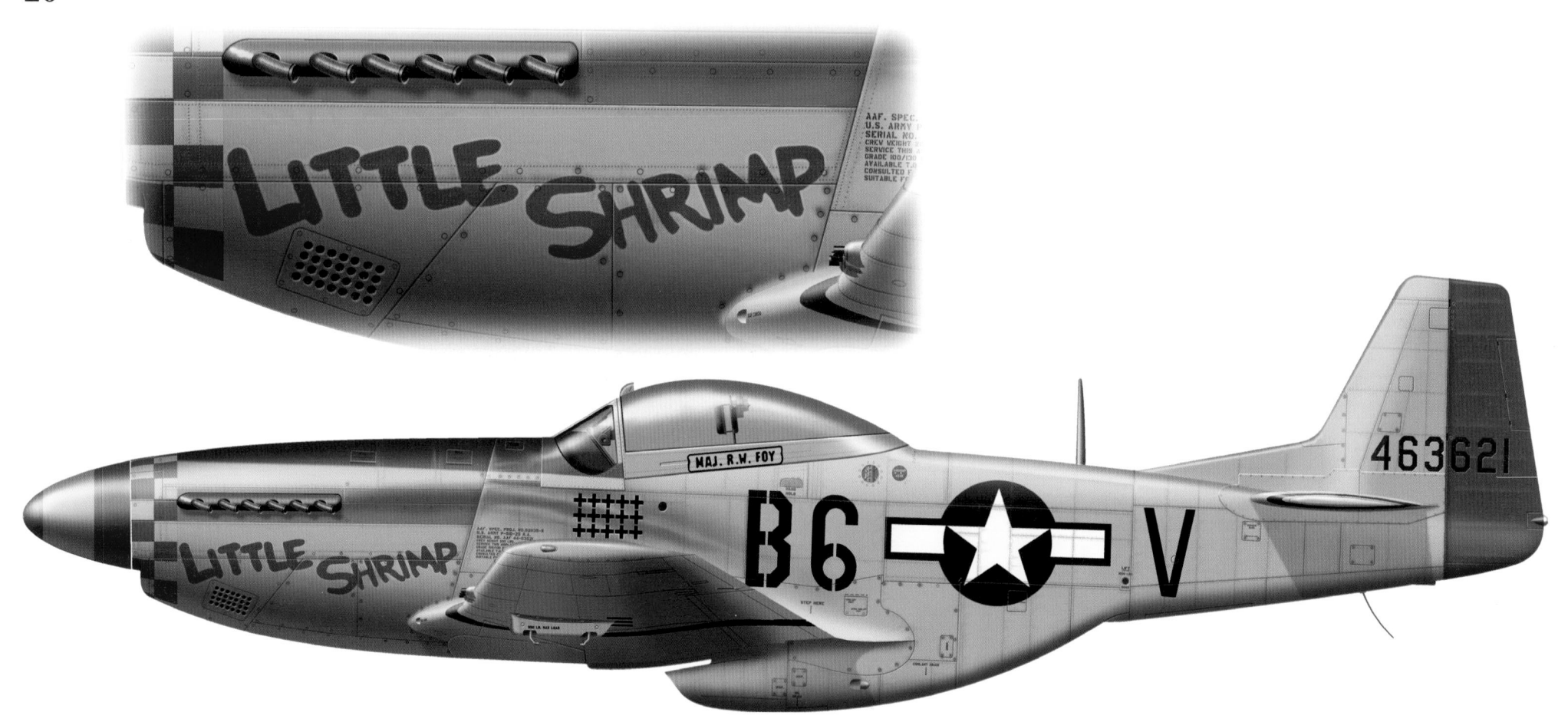

P-51D-20-NA Mustang, sn 44-63621, B6•V, 363rd FS, 357th FG, 8th AF. Leiston, UK, Winter 1944.

Maj. Robert W. Foy, P-51 air victories – 15, all air victories – 15.

Silver/natural metal overall. Anti-glare panel Olive Drab. Spinner and group markings red and yellow. Black bands on wings and horizontal stabilizer. Codes black.

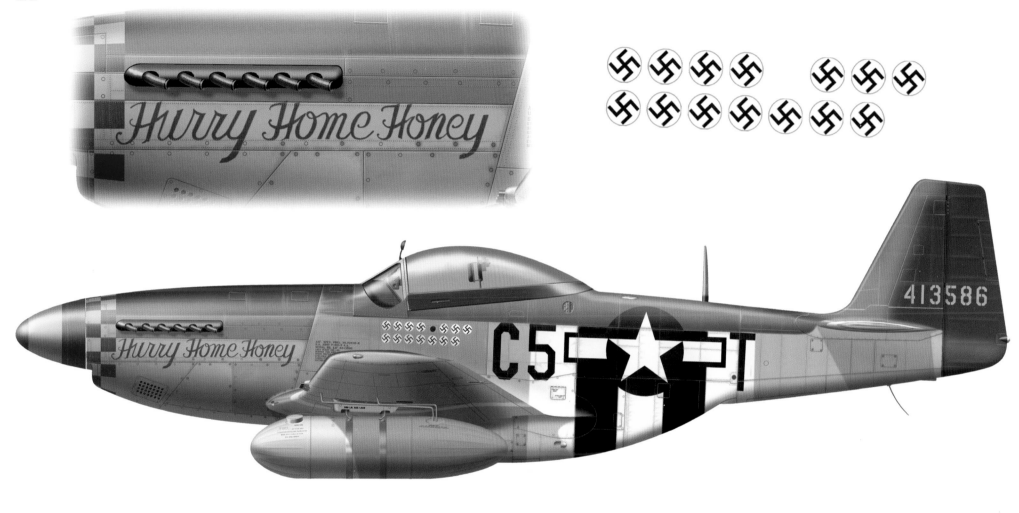

P-51D-5-NA Mustang, sn 44-13586, C5•T, 364th FS, 357th FG, 8th AF. England, Summer 1944.
Capt. Richard A. Peterson, P-51 air victories – 15.50, all air victories – 15.50.

Silver/natural metal overall. Upper surfaces Olive Drab. Spinner and group markings red and yellow. D-Day stripes on lower fuselage only.
White bands on wings horizontal stabilizer. Codes black. Serial yellow. No dorsal fin fillet.

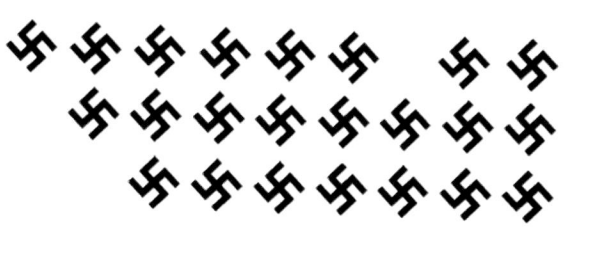

P-51D-20-NA Mustang, sn 44-63497, FT•I, 353rd FS, 354th FG, 9th AF. Paris, 1945.

Lt. Bruce W. Carr, P-51 air victories – 15, all air victories – 15.

Silver/natural metal overall. Anti-glare panel Olive Drab. Spinner and nose yellow. Black bands on wings and horizontal stabilizer. Codes black.

P-51D-10-NA Mustang, sn 44-14237, HO•W, 487th FS, 352nd FG, 8th AF. England, September 1944.

Capt. William T. Whisner, P-51 air victories – 14.50, all air victories – 15.50.

Silver/natural metal overall. Spinner, nose and rudder Medium Blue. Codes black.

P-51D-5-NT Mustang, sn 44-11280, 600, 118ᵗʰ TRS, 23ʳᵈ FG, 10ᵗʰ, 14ᵗʰ AF. China, 1945
Lt Col. Edward O. McComas, P-51 air victories – 14, all air victories – 14.
Silver/natural metal overall. Anti-glare panel Olive Drab. Spinner and lightning flashes yellow and black. Codes black.

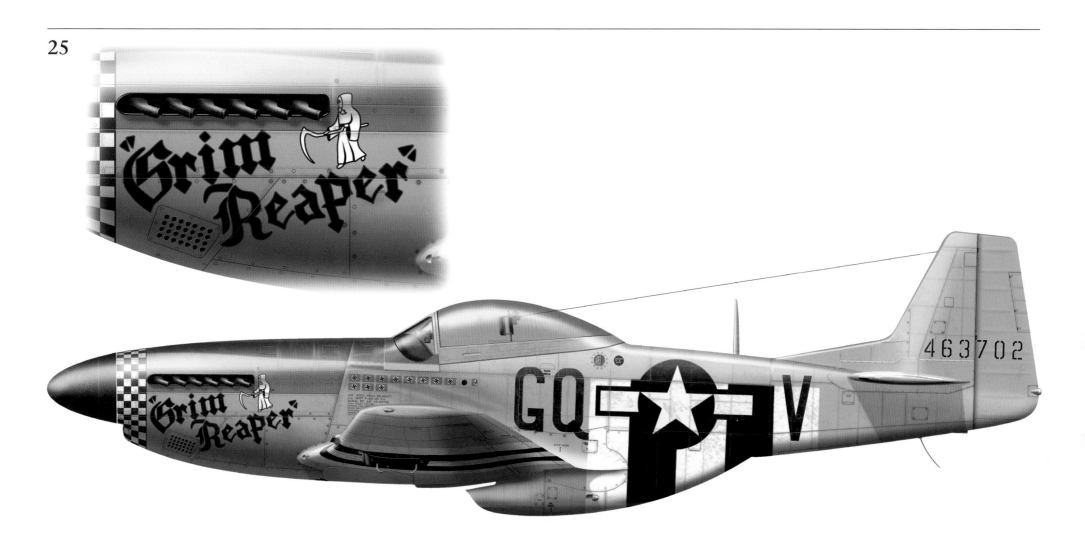

P-51D-25-NA Mustang, sn 44-63702, GQ•V, 355th FS, 354th FG, 9th AF. England, 1944.

Maj. Lowell K. Brueland, P-51 air victories – 12.50, all air victories – 12.50.

Silver/natural metal overall. Anti-glare panel Olive Drab. Spinner blue. White and blue checker. D-Day stripes on wings and fuselage.
Bands on horizontal stabilizer – white upper, black lower. Codes black.

P-51D-15-NA Mustang, sn 44-14888, B6•Y, 363ʳᵈ FS, 357ᵗʰ FG, 8ᵗʰ AF. Leiston, UK, Winter 1944.

Capt. Charles E. Yeager, P-51 air victories – 11.50, all air victories – 11.50.

Silver/natural metal overall. Anti-glare panel Olive Drab. Spinner and group markings red and yellow. Rudder red. D-Day stripes on lower fuselage only.
Black bands on wings and horizontal stabilizer. Codes black. Serial black and yellow.

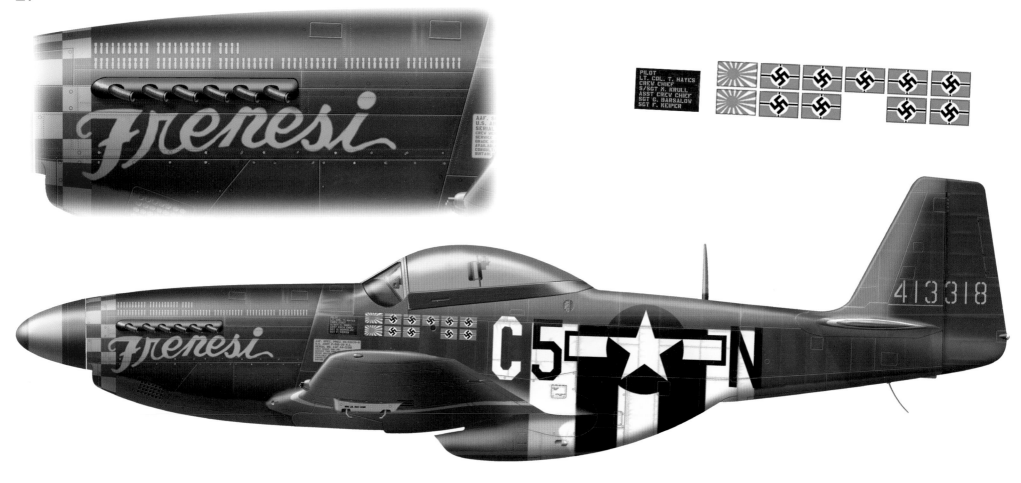

P-51D-5-NA Mustang, sn 44-13318, C5•N, 362nd FS, 357th FG, 8th AF. November 1944.

Lt. Col. Thomas L. Hayes Jr., P-51 air victories – 8.50, all air victories – 8.50.

Upper surfaces Olive Drab, under surfaces Natural Grey. Spinner and group markings red and yellow. D-Day stripes on fuselage. White bands on wings and horizontal stabilizer. Codes white and black. Serial yellow. No dorsal fin fillet.

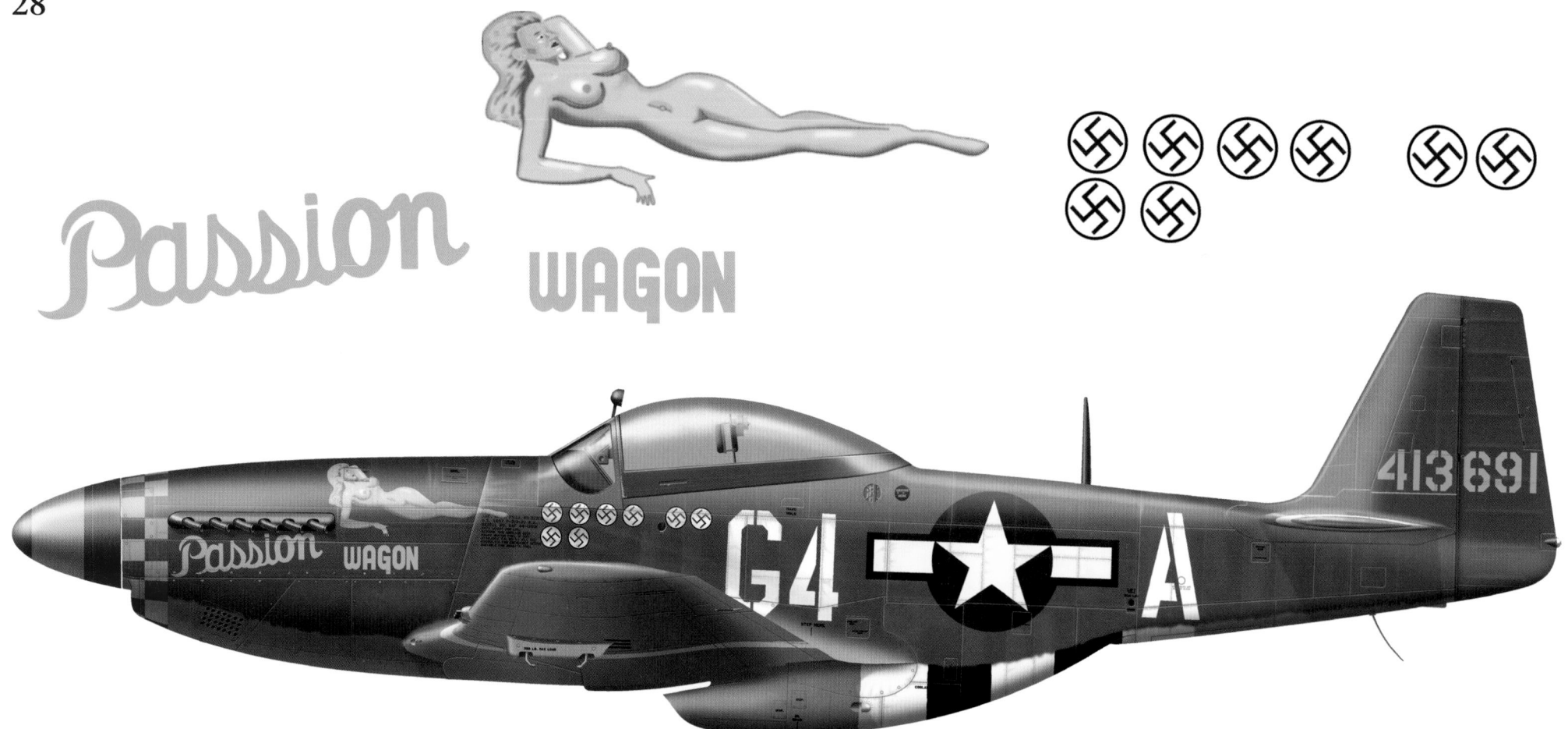

P-51D-5-NA Mustang, sn 44-13691, G4•A, 362ⁿᵈ FS, 357ᵗʰ FG, 8ᵗʰ AF. England, September 1944.

Capt. Charles E. Weaver, P-51 air victories – 8, all air victories – 8.

Upper surfaces Olive Drab, under surfaces Natural Grey. Spinner and group markings red and yellow. D-Day stripes on lower fuselage only. White bands on wings and horizontal stabilizer. Codes white. Serial yellow. No dorsal fin fillet.

P-51D-10-NA Mustang, sn 44-14292, QP•A, 4th FG, 8th AF. England, September 1944.

Lt. Col. Claiborne H. Kinnard Jr., P-51 air victories – 8, all air victories – 8.

Silver/natural metal overall. Anti-glare panel Olive Drab with red strip. D-Day stripes on wings and fuselage. Black bands on horizontal stabilizer. Upper surfaces had wavy bands of Olive Drab on wings, tail and fuselage. Codes black outlined red. Serial black.

P-51D-10-NA Mustang, sn 44-14292, QP•A, 4th FG, 8th AF.

P-51D-10-NA Mustang, sn 44-14292, QP•A, 4th FG, 8th AF.

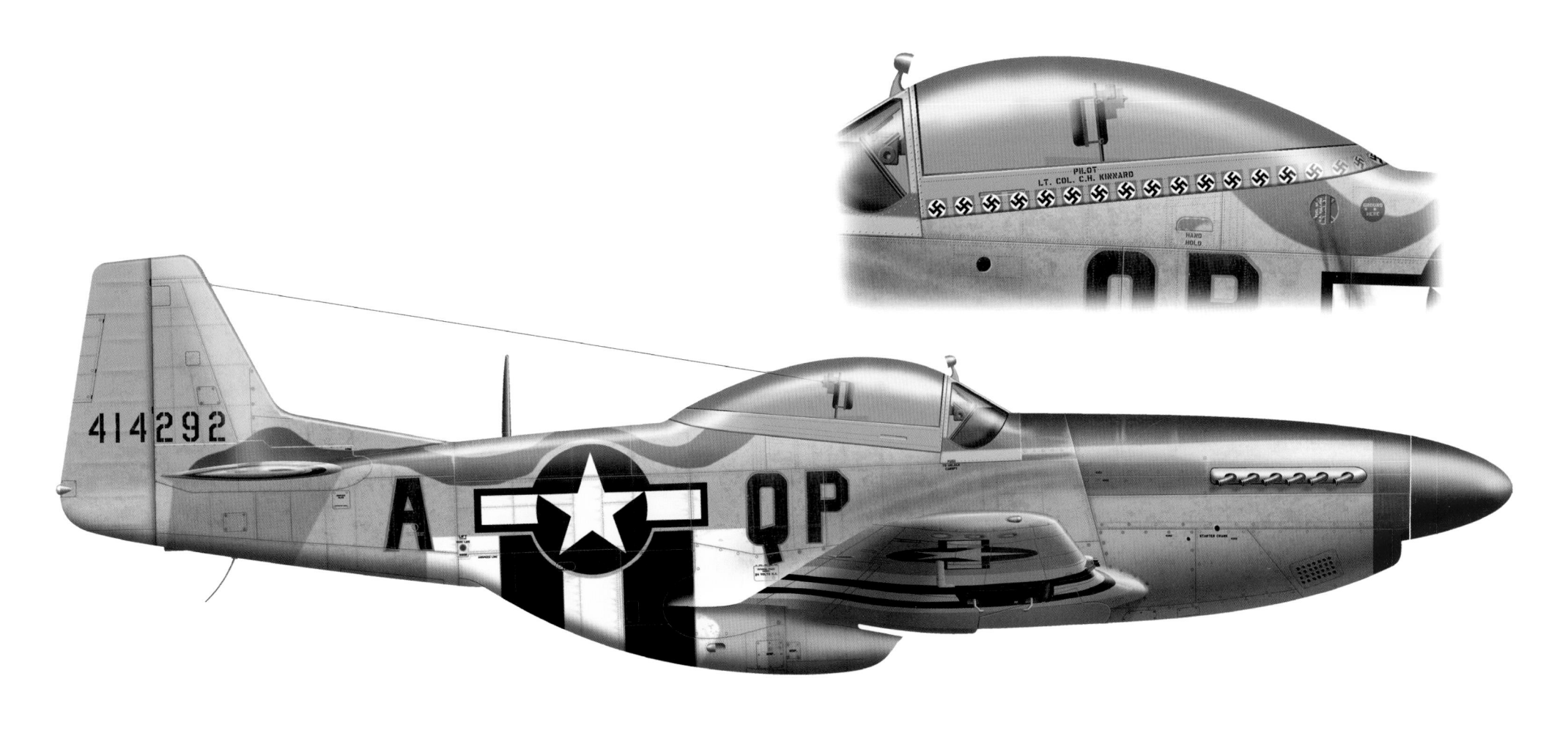

P-51D-10-NA Mustang, sn 44-14292, QP•A, 4th FG, 8th AF

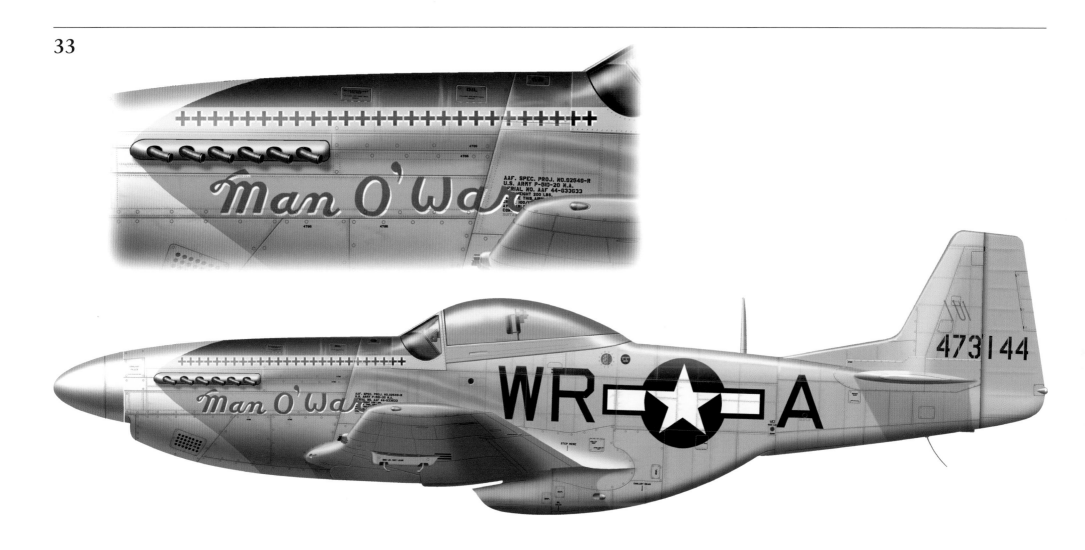

P-51D-25-NA Mustang, sn 44-73144, WR•A, 4th FG, 8th AF. England, December 1944.
Lt. Col. Claiborne H. Kinnard Jr. Group Commander, P-51 air victories – 8, all air victories – 8.
Silver/natural metal overall. Anti-glare panel Olive Drab. Spinner and nose white. Codes black.

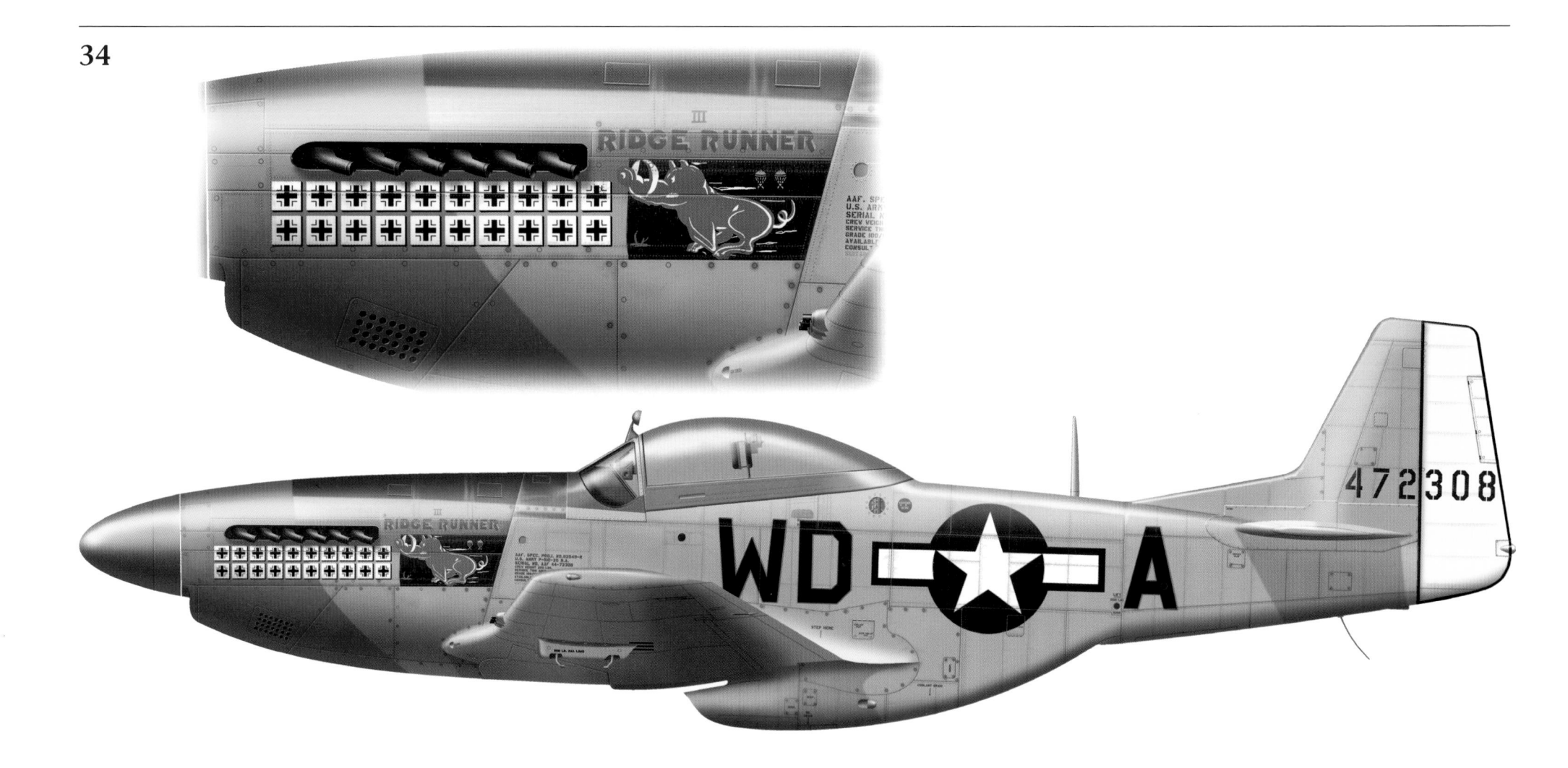

P-51D-20-NA Mustang, sn 44-72308, WD•A, 335ᵗʰ FS, 4ᵗʰ FG, 8ᵗʰ AF. April 1945.

Maj. Pierce W. McKennon, P-51 air victories – 7.50, all air victories – 12.

Silver/natural metal overall. Anti-glare panel Olive Drab. Red nose and canopy. Rudder its white with black outline. Codes black outlined red. Serial black.

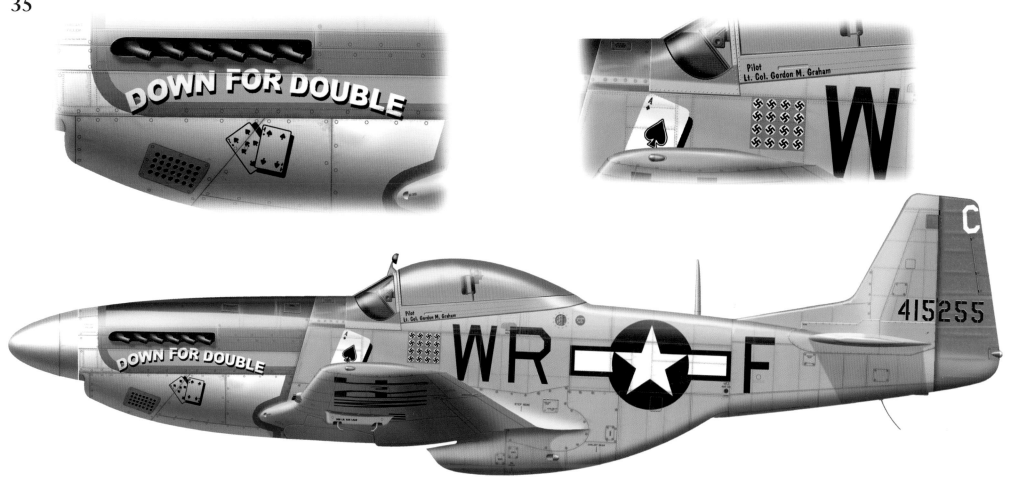

P-51D-15-NA Mustang, sn 44-15255, WR•F, 354th FS, 355th FG, 8th AF.
Lt. Col. Gordon M. Graham, P-51 air victories – 7, all air victories – 7.
Silver/natural metal overall. Anti-glare panel Olive Drab. White nose with red outline. Rudder red. Codes black.

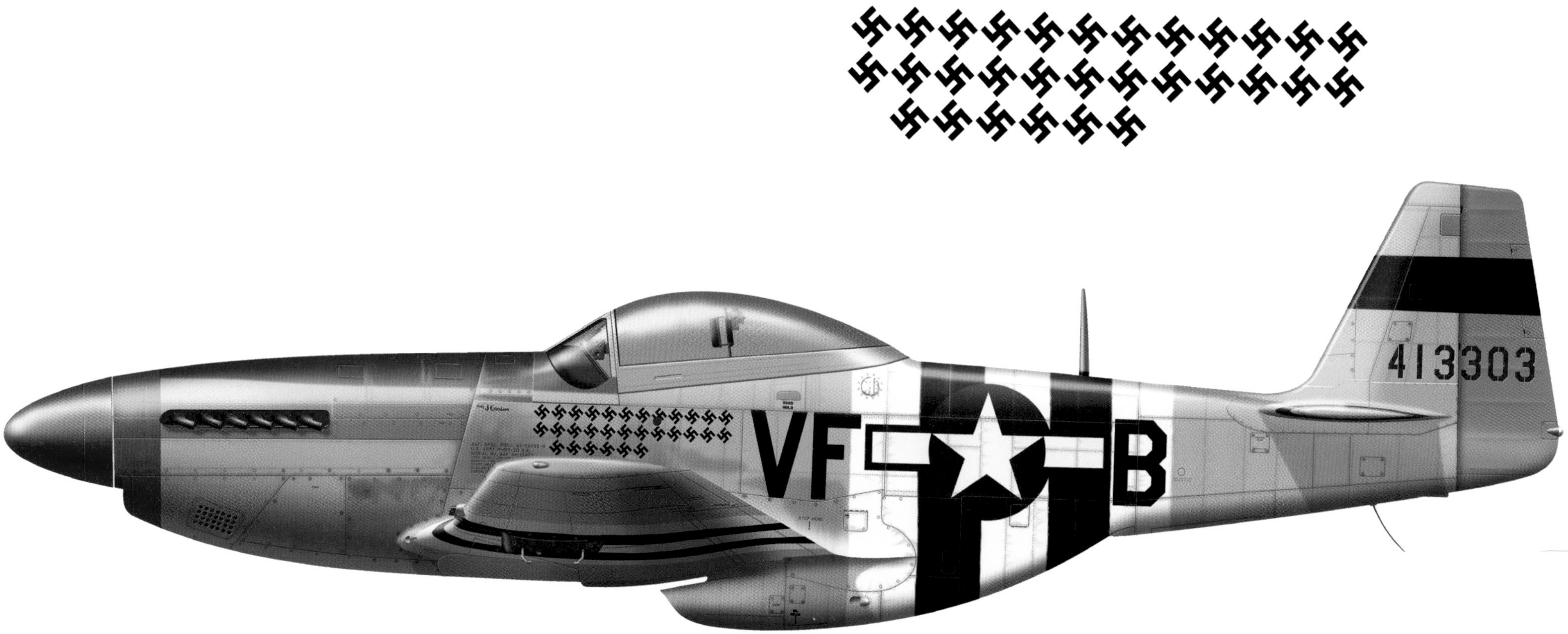

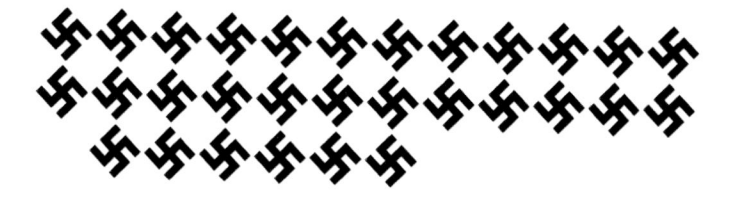

P-51D-5-NA Mustang, sn 44-13303, VF•B, 336ᵗʰ FS, 4ᵗʰ FG, 8ᵗʰ AF. England, June 1944.

Maj. James A. Goodson, P-51 air victories – 7, all air victories – 12.

Silver/natural metal overall. Anti-glare panel Olive Drab. Red nose. D-Day stripes on wings and fuselage. Rudder light blue. Codes black. No dorsal fin fillet.

P-51D-10-NA Mustang, sn 44-14140, CY•O, 343rd FS, 55th FG, 8th AF

Capt. Robert E. Welch, P-51 air victories – 6, all air victories – 6.

Silver/natural metal overall. Anti-glare panel Olive Drab with red band. Spinner and checker yellow and green. Rudder yellow. Codes black.

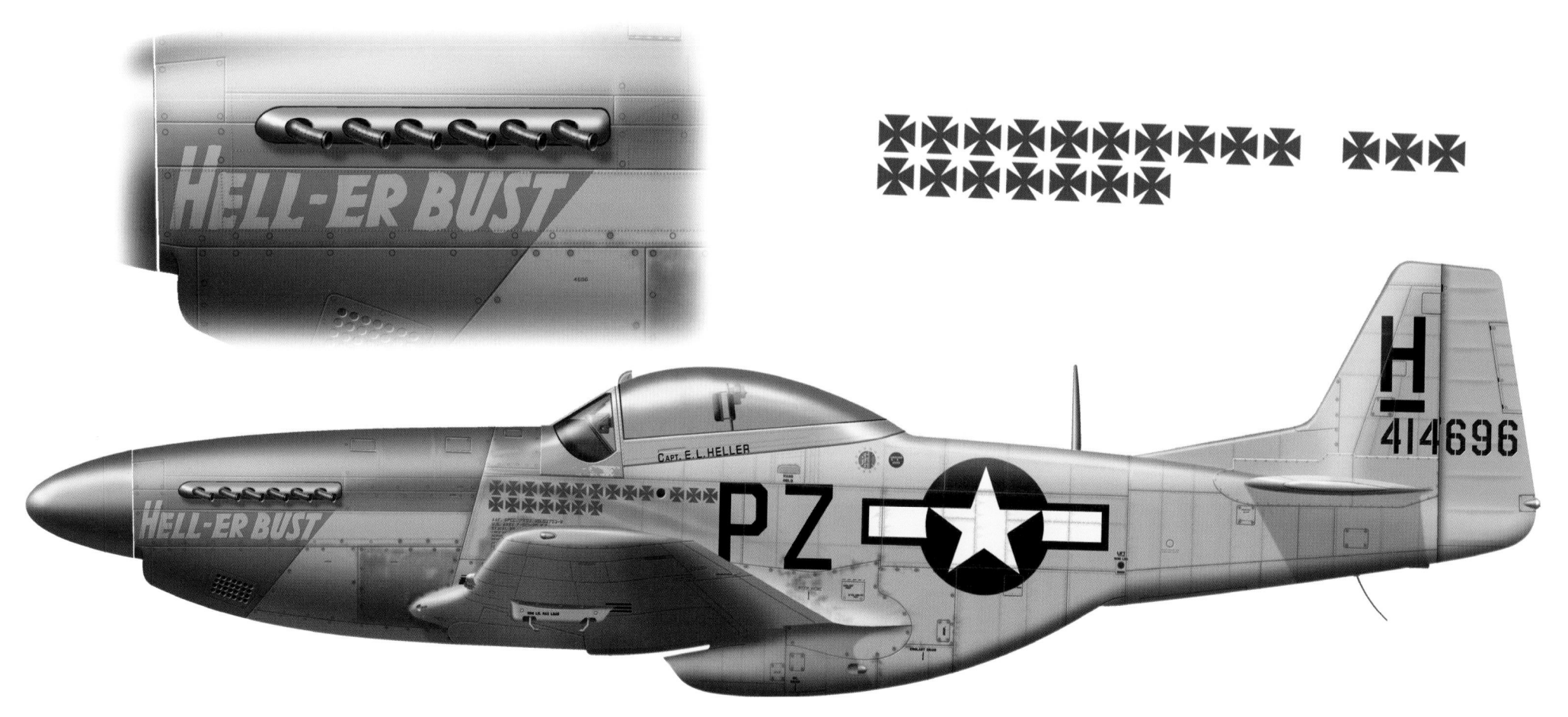

P-51D-10-NA Mustang, sn 44-14696, PZ•H, 386th FS, 352nd FG, 8th AF.
Chievres, Belgium, January 1945.
Capt. Edwin L. Heller, P-51 air victories – 5.50, all air victories – 5.50.
Silver/natural metal overall. Blue nose. Rudder yellow. Codes black.

P-51D-20-NA Mustang, sn 44-63223, QP•S, 334th FS, 4th FG, 8th AF. England, 1945.

Lt. Arthur Reed Bowers, ground strafing victories – 6.

Silver/natural metal overall. Late war red markings on nose and rudder. No black bands on wings or tail. Codes black.

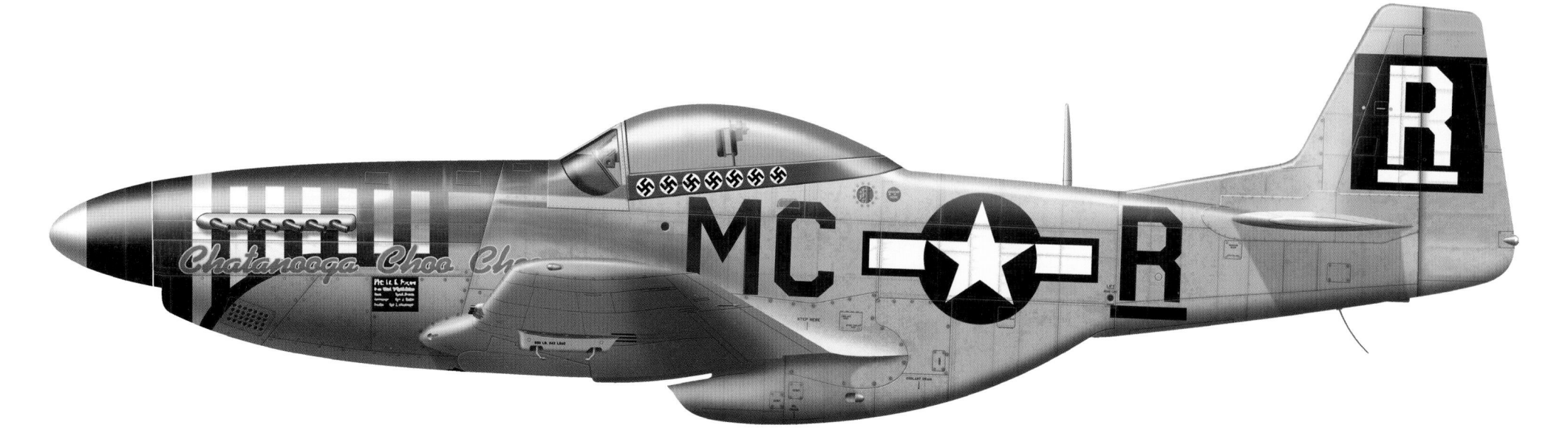

Chatanooga Choo Choo

P-51D-10-NA Mustang, sn 44-14535, MC•R, 79ᵗʰ FS, 20ᵗʰ FG, 8ᵗʰ AF. April 1945.

Lt. Edward F. Pouge, ground strafing victories – 6.

Silver/natural metal overall. Late war Group markings. The black and white stripes on the nose stand for the 20ᵗʰ Fighter Group. No stripes or bands carried. Codes black. Olive Drab canopy frame. Codes black. Note serial not marked on aircraft.

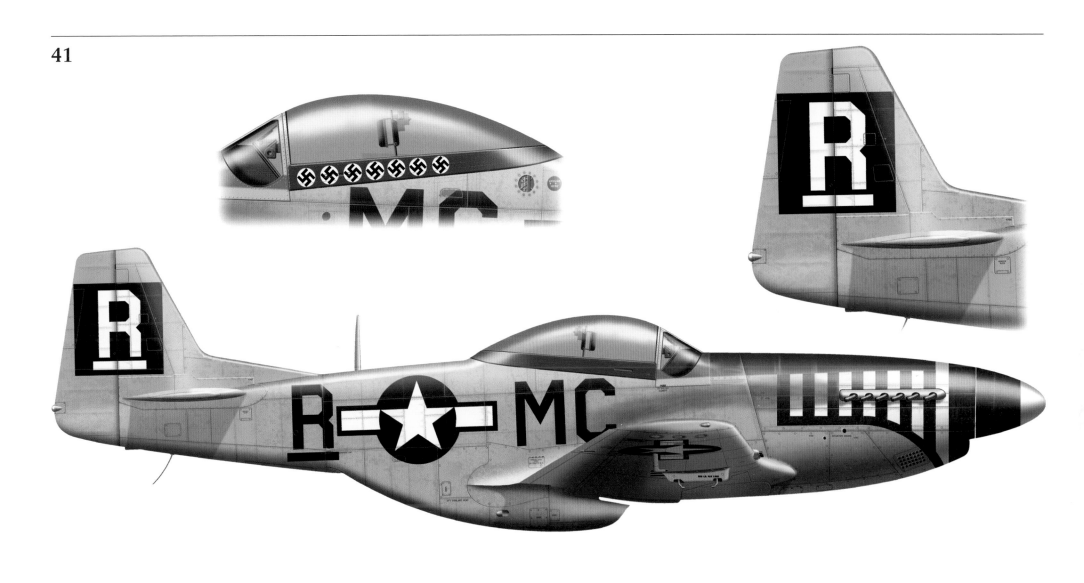

P-51D-10-NA Mustang, sn 44-14535, MC•<u>R</u>, 79th FS, 20th FG, 8th AF. April 1945.

P-51D-20-NA Mustang, sn 44-72218, WZ•I, 84th FS, 352nd FG, 8th AF. England, May 1945.

Col. John D. Landers, all air victories – 14.50, ground victories – 20.

Silver/natural metal overall. Anti-glare panel Olive Drab with red border. Spinner black, white and red. Black and white checker on nose and wings. Rudder black.

Codes black with red outline. Serial black.

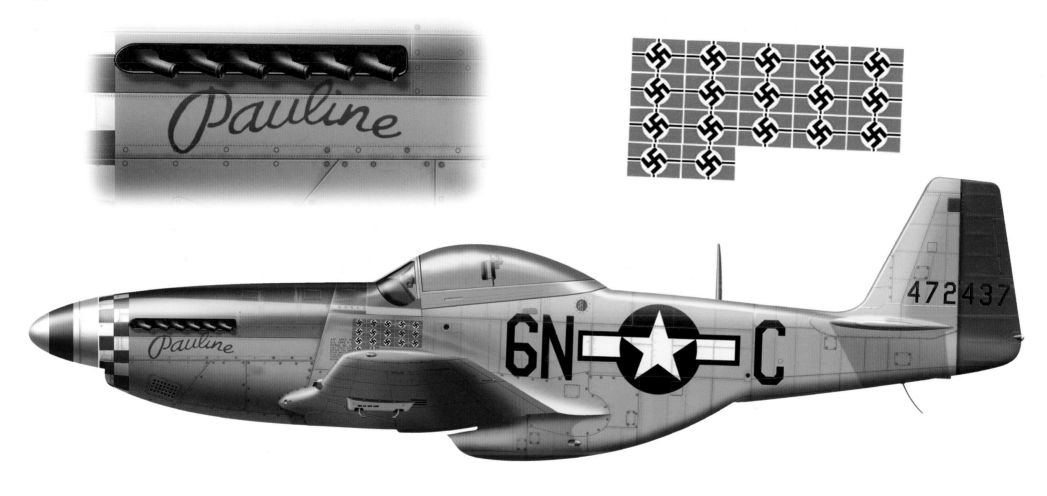

P-51D-20-NA Mustang, sn 44-72437, 6N•C, 505th FS, 352nd FG, 8th AF. Belgium, March 1945.
Lt.Col. Joseph L. Thury, all air victories – 2, ground strafing victories – 25.50.
Silver/natural metal overall. Anti-glare panel Olive Drab. White, red spinner and checker. Rudder Olive Green. Codes black. No dorsal fin fillet.

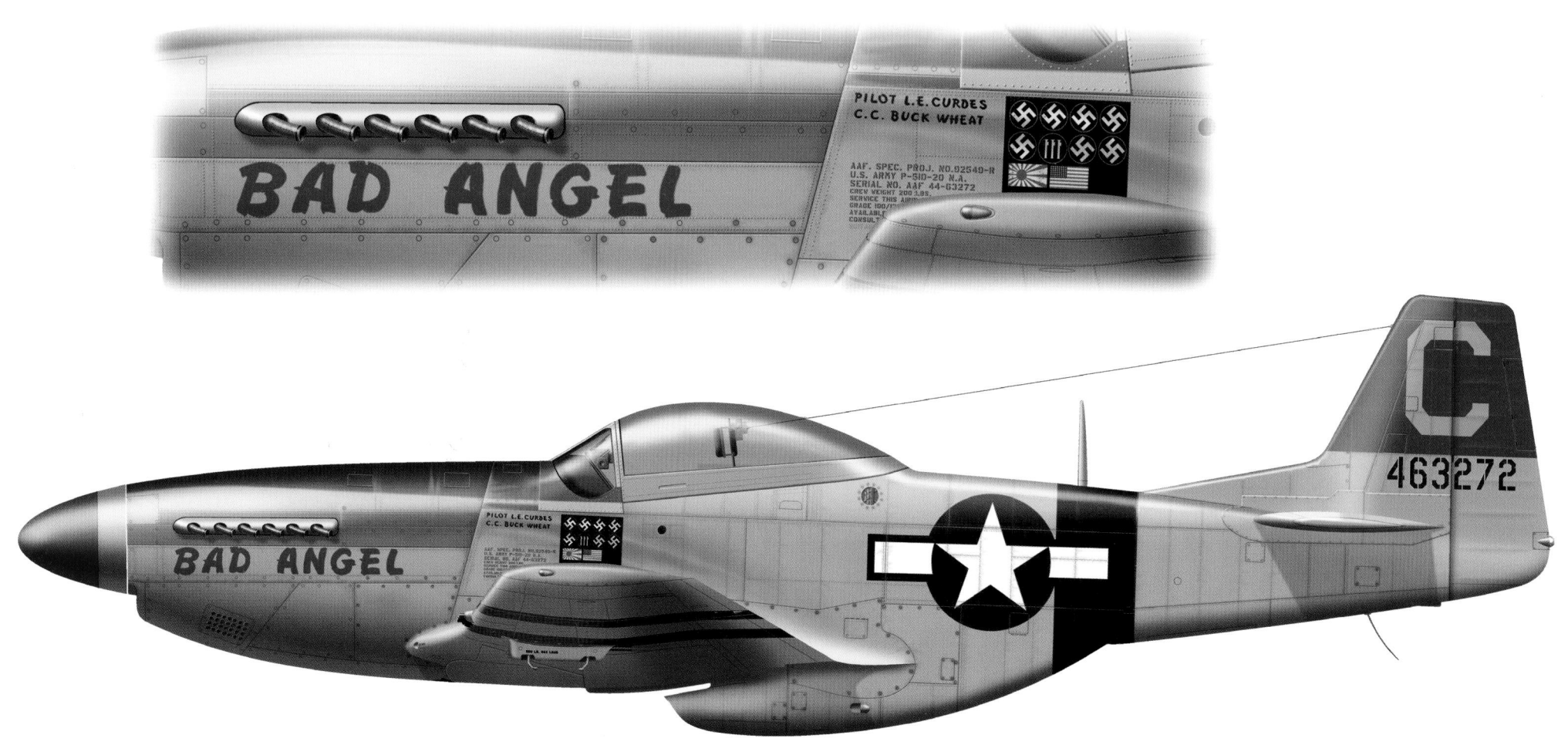

P-51D-20-NA Mustang, sn 44-63272, 4th FS, 3rd ACG (Air Commando Group). Philippines, 1945.

Lt. Louis Edward Curdes, all air victories – 10.

Curdes is one of only three Americans to have scored kills against Germany, Italy and Japan, He also shoot down an American C-47 to prevent it from landing on enemy airfield. Silver/natural metal overall. Anti-glare panel Olive Drab. Spinner red. Black stripes on wings and fuselage. Rudder light blue. Codes black.

45

Two coats of filling sprayed on and polished to obtain
a perfectly smooth surface, so that the rivets
were not visible. Airbrushed with silver paint.

One coat of filling sprayed on and polished to obtain
a perfectly smooth surface, so that the rivets
were not visible. Airbrushed with silver paint.

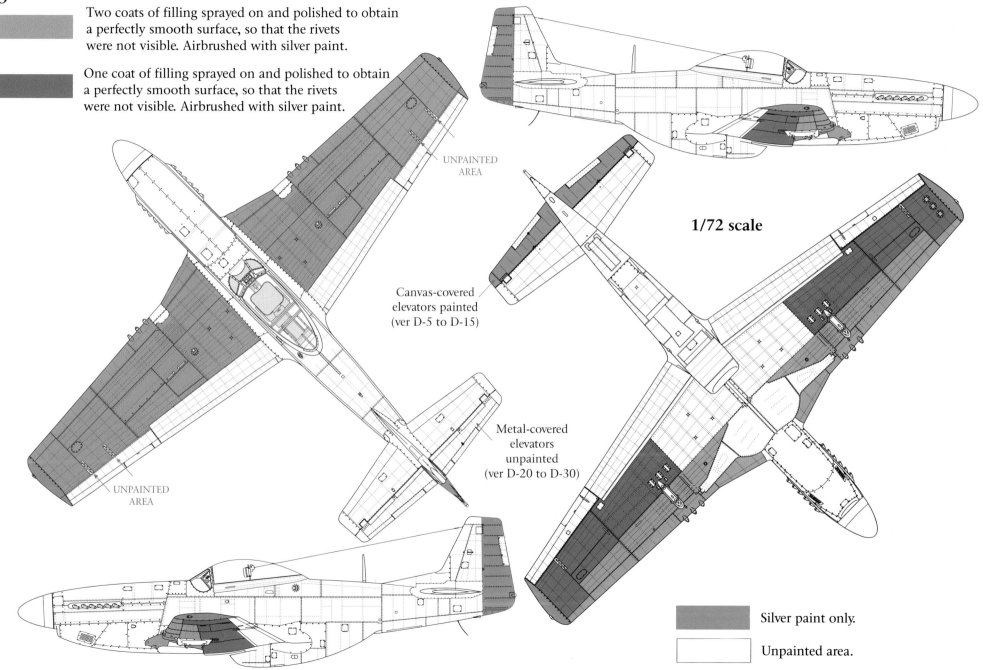

UNPAINTED AREA

UNPAINTED AREA

1/72 scale

Canvas-covered
elevators painted
(ver D-5 to D-15)

Metal-covered
elevators
unpainted
(ver D-20 to D-30)

Silver paint only.

Unpainted area.

P-51 Aces List

Name	Rank	Air Force	Group	P-51 air victories	all air victories	Profile no.
George E. Preddy Jr.	Maj.	8	352	23.83	26.83	1
John J. Voll	Capt.	15	31	21.00	21.00	2 – 5
John C. Meyer	Lt. Col.	8	352	21.00	24.00	6
Leonard K. Carson	Maj.	8	357	18.50	18.50	7 – 8
Glenn T. Eagleston	Maj.	9	354	18.50	18.50	9
John B. England	Maj.	8	357	17.50	17.50	10
James S. Varnell Jr.	Capt.	15	52	17.00	17.00	11
Ray S. Wetmore	Capt.	8	359	17.00	21.25	16
Don S. Gentile	Capt.	8	4	16.50	21.83	12
Clarence E. Anderson Jr.	Capt.	8	357	16.25	16.25	13 – 14
Samuel J. Brown	Maj.	15	31	15.50	15.50	
Richard A. Peterson	Capt.	8	357	15.50	15.50	21
Don M. Beerbower	Capt.	9	354	15.50	15.50	
Robert W. Foy	Maj.	8	357	15.00	15.00	15, 17 – 20
Jack T. Bradley	Lt. Col.	9	354	15.00	15.00	
Bruce W. Carr	Lt.	9	363, 354	15.00	15.00	22
William T. Whisner	Capt.	8	352	14.50	15.50	23
Henry W. Brown	Capt.	8	355	14.20	14.20	
John C. Herbst	Maj.	10, 14	23	14.00	18.00	
Edward O. McComas	Lt. Col.	10, 14	23	14.00	14.00	24
Wallace N. Emmer	Capt.	9	354	14.00	14.00	
Donald H. Bochkay	Maj.	8	357	13.83	13.83	
John T. Godfrey	Capt.	8	4	13.83	16.33	
James L. Brooks	Lt.	15	31	13.00	13.00	
Harry A. Parker	Capt.	15	325	13.00	13.00	
Robert C. Curtis	Maj.	15	52	13.00	14.00	
Ralph K. Hofer	Lt.	8	4	13.00	15.00	
Clyde B. East	Capt.	9	15 TRS	13.00	13.00	
Robert W. Stephens	Maj.	9	354	13.00	13.00	
George Carpenter	Maj.	8	4	12.83	12.83	
Lowell K. Brueland	Maj.	9	354	12.50	12.50	25
Norman C. Skogstad	Lt.	15	31	12.00	12.00	
Glennon T. Moran	Lt.	8	352	12.00	13.00	
Nicholas Megura	Capt.	8	4	11.83	11.83	
John A. Kirla	Lt.	8	357	11.50	11.50	
Charles E. Yeager	Capt.	8	357	11.50	11.50	26
Robert J. Goebel	Capt.	15	31	11.00	11.00	
Robert E. Riddle	Lt.	15	31	11.00	11.00	
Wayne L. Lowry	Lt.	15	325	11.00	11.00	
J. Barry Lawler	Capt.	15	52	11.00	11.00	
Robert W. Moore	Maj.	7	15	11.00	12.00	
John F. Thornell Jr.	Lt.	8	352	11.00	17.25	
Howard D. Hively	Maj.	8	4	11.00	12.00	
Kenneth H. Dahlberg	Capt.	9	354	11.00	14.00	
Carl M. Frantz	Lt.	9	354	11.00	11.00	
Richard E. Turner	Maj.	9	354	11.00	11.00	
Frank Q. O'Connor	Capt.	9	354	10.75	10.75	
Raymond H. Littge	Capt.	8	352	10.50	10.50	
Donald J. Strait	Maj.	8	356	10.50	13.50	
John A. Storch	Lt. Col.	8	357	10.50	10.50	
Fred W. Glover	Maj.	8	4	10.30	10.30	
James J. England	Maj.	10, 14	311	10.00	10.00	
Walter J. Goehausen Jr.	Capt.	15	31	10.00	10.00	
Wayne K. Blickenstaff	Lt. Col.	8	353	10.00	10.00	
Ted E. Lines	Capt.	8	4	10.00	10.00	
Willard W. Millikan	Capt.	8	4	10.00	13.00	
Arthur F. Jeffrey	Lt. Col.	8	479	10.00	14.00	
William J. Hovde	Maj.	8	355	9.50	10.50	
Dale F. Spencer	Lt.	8	361	9.50	9.50	
Fletcher E. Adams	Capt.	8	357	9.00	9.00	
William R. Beyer	Capt.	8	361	9.00	9.00	
George F. Ceuleers	Lt. Col.	8	364	9.00	10.50	
Charles F. Anderson	Lt.	8	4	9.00	10.00	
Louis H. Norley	Maj.	8	4	9.00	10.30	
George W. Gleason	Capt.	8	479	9.00	12.00	
Loyd J. Overfield	Lt.	9	354	9.00	11.00	
Frederick J. Dorsch Jr.	Capt.	15	31	8.50	8.50	
Ernest C. Fiebelkorn	Capt.	8	20	8.50	9.00	
Charles J. Cesky	Capt.	8	352	8.50	8.50	
Carl J. Luksic	Lt.	8	352	8.50	8.50	
Sanford K. Moats	Lt.	8	352	8.50	8.50	
Thomas L. Hayes Jr.	Lt. Col.	8	357	8.50	8.50	27
Otto D. Jenkins	Lt.	8	357	8.50	8.50	
George A. Doersch	Capt.	8	359	8.50	10.50	
Ernest E. Bankey Jr.	Capt.	8	364	8.50	9.50	
John H. Hoefker	Capt.	9	15 TRS	8.50	8.50	
Don McDowell	Lt.	9	354	8.50	8.50	
Charles H. Older	Lt. Col.	10, 14	23	8.00	18.00	
Victor E. Warford	Maj.	15	31	8.00	8.00	
Arthur C. Fiedler Jr.	Capt.	15	325	8.00	8.00	
Philip Sangermano	Lt.	15	325	8.00	8.00	
William A. Shomo	Capt.	5	82 TRS	8.00	8.00	
Francis R. Gerard	Capt.	8	339	8.00	8.00	
Joseph E. Broadhead	Maj.	8	357	8.00	8.00	
Robert M. Shaw	Lt.	8	357	8.00	8.00	
John L. Sublett	Capt.	8	357	8.00	8.00	
Charles E. Weaver	Capt.	8	357	8.00	8.00	28
James M. Fowle	Capt.	8	364	8.00	8.00	
Claiborne H. Kinnard Jr.	Lt. Col.	8	4,355	8.00	8.00	29 – 33
Robin Olds	Maj.	8	479	8.00	13.00	
Joseph L. Lang	Capt.	8	4	7.83	7.83	
William T. Halton	Maj.	8	352	7.50	8.50	
Henry J. Miklajcyk	Capt.	8	352	7.50	7.50	
Glendon v. Davis	Capt.	8	357	7.50	7.50	

Name	Rank	Air Force	Group	P-51 air victories	all air victories	Profile no.
Dale E. Karger	Lt.	8	357	7.50	7.50	
Donald J.M. Blakeslee	Col.	8	4	7.50	15.50	
Bernard L. McGrattan	Capt.	8	4	7.50	8.50	
Pierce W. McKennon	Maj.	8	4	7.50	12.00	34
Albert L. Schlegel	Capt.	8	4	7.50	8.50	
Elwyn G. Righetti	Lt. Col.	8	55	7.50	7.50	
George M. Lamb	Maj.	9	354	7.50	7.50	
Charles W. Lasko	Capt.	9	354	7.50	7.50	
Robert M. Goodnight	Lt.	9	354	7.25	7.25	
Murray D. McLaughlin	Capt.	15	31	7.00	7.00	
Ernest Shipman	Lt.	15	31	7.00	7.00	
Robert H. Brown	Lt.	15	325	7.00	7.00	
John M. Simmons	Lt.	15	325	7.00	7.00	
Calvin D. Allen Jr.	Lt.	15	52	7.00	7.00	
Duane R. Franklin	Lt.	15	52	7.00	7.00	
Daniel J. Zoerb	Capt.	15	52	7.00	7.00	
Stephen W. Andrew	Maj.	8	352	7.00	8.00	
Donald S. Bryan	Capt.	8	352	7.00	13.30	
John L. Elder Jr.	Maj.	8	355	7.00	8.00	
Gordon M. Graham	Lt. Col.	8	355	7.00	7.00	35
Bert W. Marshall Jr.	Maj.	8	355	7.00	7.00	
Robert E. Woody	Capt.	8	355	7.00	7.00	
Robert H. Becker	Capt.	8	357	7.00	7.00	
James W. Browning	Capt.	8	357	7.00	7.00	
John B. Carder	Lt.	8	357	7.00	7.00	
Gilbert M. O'Brien	Lt.	8	357	7.00	7.00	
Joseph F. Pierce	Lt.	8	357	7.00	7.00	
Gerald E. Tyler	Lt.	8	357	7.00	7.00	
Niven K. Cranfill	Maj.	8	359	7.00	7.00	
Gilbert L. Jamison	Capt.	8	364	7.00	7.00	
James A. Goodson	Maj.	8	4	7.00	12.00	36
William H. Lewis	Capt.	8	55	7.00	7.00	
William Y. Anderson	Lt.	9	354	7.00	7.00	
James B. Dalglish	Maj.	9	354	7.00	9.00	
Robert Reynolds	Lt.	9	354	7.00	7.00	
F. Michael Rogers	Capt.	9	354	7.00	7.00	
James E. Hoffman Jr.	Lt.	15	52	6.50	6.50	
Arthur G. Johnson Jr.	Lt.	15	52	6.50	8.50	
Ralph L. Cox	Capt.	8	359	6.50	6.50	
Valentine S. Rader	Lt.	9	111 TRS	6.50	6.50	
Edward E. Hunt	Lt.	9	354	6.50	6.50	
Charles B. Koenig	Lt.	9	354	6.50	6.50	
Robert D. Welden	Lt.	9	354	6.25	6.25	
Lester L. Arasmith	Lt.	10, 14	311	6.00	6.00	
Leonard R. Reeves	Lt.	10, 14	311	6.00	6.00	
John M. Ainley	Lt.	15	31	6.00	6.00	
George T. Buck	Capt.	15	31	6.00	6.00	
William J. Dillard	Capt.	15	31	6.00	6.00	

Name	Rank	Air Force	Group	P-51 air victories	all air victories	Profile no.
Charles M. McCorkle	Col.	15	31	6.00	11.00	
Leland P. Molland	Capt.	15	31	6.00	10.50	
David C. Wilhelm	Capt.	15	31	6.00	6.00	
Barrie S. Davis	Lt.	15	325	6.00	6.00	
Gordon H. McDaniel	Lt.	15	325	6.00	6.00	
William F. Hanes Jr.	Lt.	15	52	6.00	6.00	
Robert A. Karr	Capt.	15	52	6.00	6.00	
James O. Tyler	Capt.	15	52	6.00	8.00	
James B. Tapp	Maj.	7	15	6.00	8.00	
Harry C. Crim Jr.	Maj.	7	21	6.00	6.00	
Harley L. Brown	Lt.	8	20	6.00	6.00	
Donald A. Larson	Maj.	8	339	6.00	6.00	
James R. Starnes	Capt.	8	339	6.00	6.00	
Willie O. Jackson	Lt. Col.	8	352	6.00	7.00	
Walter E. Starck	Capt.	8	352	6.00	7.00	
Everett W. Stewart	Col.	8	352, 355	6.00	7.83	
Henry S. Bille	Maj.	8	355	6.00	6.00	
Fred R. Haviland Jr.	Capt.	8	355	6.00	6.00	
Andrew J. Evans Jr.	Lt. Col.	8	357	6.00	6.00	
John F. Pugh	Capt.	8	357	6.00	6.00	
Arval J. Roberson	Lt.	8	357	6.00	6.00	
Robert G. Schimanski	Capt.	8	357	6.00	6.00	
Cyril W. Jones Jr.	Lt.	8	359	6.00	6.00	
Urban L. Drew	Lt.	8	361	6.00	6.00	
William T. Kemp	Lt.	8	361	6.00	6.00	
James A. Clark Jr.	Lt. Col	8	4	6.00	10.50	
Paul S. Riley	Lt.	8	4	6.00	6.50	
William E. Whalen	Lt.	8	4, 2 SF	6.00	6.00	
Richard G. Candelaria	Lt.	8	479	6.00	6.00	
Donald M. Cummings	Capt.	8	55	6.00	6.00	
Bernard H. Howes	Lt.	8	55	6.00	6.00	
Robert E. Welch	Capt.	8	55	6.00	6.00	37
Leland A. Larson	Lt.	9	15 TRS	6.00	6.00	
Warren S. Emerson	Capt.	9	354	6.00	6.00	
Clayton K. Gross	Capt.	9	354	6.00	6.00	
Charles F. Gumm	Lt.	9	354	6.00	6.00	
James H. Howard	Col.	9	354	6.00	9.00	
William J. Simmons	Lt.	9	354	6.00	6.00	
Richard C. Lampe	Lt.	15	52	5.50	5.50	
Edwin L. Heller	Capt.	8	352	5.50	5.50	38
Arthur C. Cundy	Lt.	8	353	5.50	7.50	
William J. Cullerton	Lt.	8	355	5.50	5.50	
Norman J. Fortier	Capt.	8	355	5.50	5.83	
Charles W. Lenfest	Capt.	8	355	5.50	5.50	
Lelsie D. Minchew	Capt.	8	355	5.50	5.50	
Clinton D. Burdick	Lt.	8	356	5.50	5.50	
Frank L. Gailer Jr.	Lt.	8	357	5.50	5.50	
Paul R. Hatala	Capt.	8	357	5.50	5.50	

Published in Poland in 2015
by STRATUS s.c.
Po. Box 123,
27-600 Sandomierz 1, Poland
e-mail: office@mmpbooks.biz
for
Mushroom Model Publications,
3 Gloucester Close,
Petersfield,
Hampshire GU32 3AX
e-mail: rogerw@mmpbooks.biz

© 2015 Mushroom Model
Publications.
http://www.mmpbooks.biz

ISBN

978-83-63678-79-1

Editor in chief
Roger Wallsgrove

Editorial Team
Bartłomiej Belcarz
Robert Pęczkowski
Artur Juszczak

Colour profiles
Artur Juszczak

DTP
Artur Juszczak

Printed by
Drukarnia Diecezjalna,
ul. Żeromskiego 4,
27-600 Sandomierz
www.wds.pl
marketing@wds.pl

Selected Bibliography

Campbell John M. & Campbell Donna, *P-51 Mustang Nose Art Gallery*, Motorbooks Intl, 1994

Dorr, Robert F.. *P-51 Mustang (Warbird History)*: St. Paul, Minnesota: Motorbooks International Publishers, 1995. ISBN 0-7603-0002-X.

Ethell, Jeffrey L. *P-51 Mustang: In Color, Photos from World War II and Korea*: St. Paul, Minnesota: Motorbooks International Publishers & Wholesalers, 1993. ISBN 0-87938-818-8.

Johnsen, Frederick A. *North American P-51 Mustang (Warbird Tech Series, Vol. 5)*: Speciality Press, 1997

Karnas, Dariusz. *P-51D Mustang*. Modelmania 3, Gdańsk (Poland): AJ-Press, 2005

Kinzey, Bert. *P-51 Mustang in Detail & Scale: Part 2; P-51D thu P-82H*: Carrollton, Texas: Detail & Scale Inc., 1997. ISBN 1-888974-03-6

Kolacha, Zbigniew and Żurek, Jacek, B. *North American P-51 Mustang, P-82 Twin Mustang*: Gdańsk (Poland): AJ-Press, 1999

Ludwig, Paul A. and Tullis Tom, *P-51 Mustang: Development of the Long-Range Escort Fighter*: Classic Publications, 2003

Matysiak, Paweł. *North American P-51D/K Mustang and Cavalier F-51D Conversion*: Lublin (Poland): Kagero, 2011

Money, Barry and Money, Ann. *The Warlords vol. 1 The 4th, 20th & 55th Fighter Group*. Ottringham (Great Britain): Flight Recorder Publications Ltd, 2003

O'Leary, Michael, *NAA P-51 Mustang   Production Line to Frontline*, Osprey Publishing

Pęczkowski, Robert. *North American P-51D Mustang*. Sandomierz (Poland): MMPBooks, 2009

Scutts, Jerry. *Mustang Aces of the Eighth Air Force*, Osprey Publishing

Styling, Mark, Scutts, Jerry. Mustang Aces of the 9th, 15th Air Forces & RAF, Osprey Publishing

Szlagor, Tomasz. *P-51D/K Mustangi nad III Rzeszą*. Lublin: Kagero, 2008

Szlagor, Tomasz, Światłoń, Janusz, Wieliczko, Leszek, A. *Fighters over Japan*: Topcolors 3: Lublin (Poland): Kagero, 2007

PRINTED IN POLAND